STILL STANDING

'Tola has confronted life's "failures" head on and writes honestly about her feelings and responses to the difficulties she has faced. Books by Christians are rarely so authentic and raw. Drawing wisdom from the Bible, she turns these "failures" into lessons to learn from, with short, punchy chapters which have a devotional quality, pointing readers to a loving, gracious God.'
Catherine Butcher

'Tola has a gift for weaving Scripture and her real-life experiences together. Her down-to-earth approach and vulnerability will really resonate with readers.'
Ronke Lawal

'This book is an honest, vulnerable look at living in the real world. Tola may have "seethed" the first time someone suggested her experiences would be able to help many, but this book is a testament to the fact that her friend's comment, however unwelcome at the time, was totally right. I have known and loved Tola through just some of her ups and downs, but time and again I have seen her wrestle with her challenges and find God in their midst. God so often doesn't look like we expect or turn up in the way we want, Tola's gift is to hear his voice above the melee and to look with fresh eyes at the world. I hope that as you read this book, it helps you to do just the same.'
Bekah Legg

'If you're tired of people peddling unachievable goals and unreal expectations, this book will be a breath of fresh air. Tola's honesty and clarity is a tonic; her story is an empowering example of how we can live imperfect but beautiful lives. We know the truth sets us free, and I thank God for this book, which is packed full of God's insight and freedom.'
Cathy Madavan

'A memoir of raw honesty and resilient faith. I loved it.'
Jo Saxton

STILL STANDING

100 Lessons from an
'Unsuccessful' Life

Tola Doll Fisher

First published in Great Britain in 2020

Society for Promoting Christian Knowledge
36 Causton Street
London SW1P 4ST
www.spck.org.uk

British Library Cataloguing-in-Publication Data
A catalogue record for this book is available from the British Library

ISBN 978–0–281–08325–1
eBook ISBN 978–0–281–08326–8

Typeset by Nord Compo
First printed in Great Britain by Ashford Colour Press

eBook by Nord Compo

Produced on paper from sustainable forests

Contents

Contents

Section Three
Lessons from friendship

Section Four
Lessons from family

Contents

Section Five
Lessons from marriage

Section Six
Lessons from loss

Section Seven
Lessons from identity

Contents

Section Eight
Lessons from dating

Section Nine
Lessons from health

Contents

Section Ten
Lessons from standing

Introduction

I was 29, living in a flatshare in London, drunk texting my almost ex-husband to try to get him to sleep with me again. I missed him so much it was painful, but this was a record low. God had 'let' my daughter die and my marriage fall apart, so I hadn't been to church in months. I was barely functioning at work and found myself wondering: how had I gone from having everything to suddenly losing it all?

My plan was to be married with three children by the time I was 24. I loved boys, children and entertaining; I was ambitious too. The perfect poster girl for a promising future – professional highs alongside domestic success. As it happens, I was engaged at 24, married at 26, bereaved of our child at 28 and divorced by 30. So far, so *not* according to plan.

As a perfectionist – and a Christian – this felt like failure on an immeasurable scale. In church, where a woman's 'Sunday Best' is too often having the perfect nuclear family, people would frequently ask if I 'had a family'. Apparently, my parents and siblings didn't count. As a millennial, I'm surrounded by messages that suggest societal expectations for women have changed, but for Christians, the age-old message can often feel the same: get married, have babies, live a great life! But even if you do 'get there', is 'there' where we find contentment?

As a journalist, writing has always been therapeutic for me, and this book is born out of journals from my 'wilderness years' – years during which the lessons from my testimony have really taken place. Divorced and childless, I had well-meaning friends who encouraged me that when I remarried or had another baby, things would feel completely different. But God does not want us to wait until we have what we (think we) want to live the amazing life he has for us. There's a scripture in John 10.10 in which Jesus says, 'The thief comes only to steal and kill and destroy. I came that you might have life and have it more abundantly.' This is a lifestyle I truly believe in and am learning to live by, not because of who I am or what I have, but because of who God says I am and what he has for me.

Recently one of my friends said that she loved how I celebrate myself. At first, I was offended; was she saying that I was a show-off? In reality, she was actually talking about the way I live. I dance on tables, wear my best lingerie every day, pop bottles of champagne at any and every opportunity, and love God through it all – admittedly, some days better than others. It is not because I'm fancy. It's because God has shown me that despite the pain, life is full of opportunities to live an abundant, joyful life. Life is a gift from God, and if we look hard enough, there is always something to celebrate. So whatever situation you find yourself in, I hope that as I share some of the things God has taught and continues to teach me, these bruised and broken, sometimes completely bonkers, accounts will encourage you to live that John 10.10, full of abundant life that God came to give. My prayer for you is that no matter how many knocks you take, you will find yourself still standing.

Acknowledgements

Two years ago, after pitching it to more than 100 publishers and literary agents, it was Philip Law, SPCK's Publishing Director who saw the potential in *Still Standing* and sent it on to my wonderful editor Elizabeth Neep. After reading my hard won manuscript, she said, 'This is a great first draft!' Thank you Elizabeth for championing my writing and showing me how the book process works, and to SPCK for giving me the 'yes' I had been searching for.

Mum taught me to read and write and I recognize that without her early intervention, the trajectory of my life could have gone very differently. Love you Mumma. To my dear friend Valerie Jeannis, I'm amazed that you believed in me so much that you sent me a guide on how to write a book, long before I put pen to paper. I'll never forget that. There are many people who have encouraged and supported not just my writing journey but also my life and there isn't enough space to list everyone here (blame my editor for the one page limit!). But I want to mention a few of those who really pushed me as I slow jogged towards the finish line by listening to me moan, reading my drafts and being first in line to buy *Still Standing* when it was finally available IRL: Pops, Oyinda Fakeye, Teiko Dornor-Tagoe, Rachael Anderson, Laura Freedman, Karen Sibindi, Kunmi Olatunji, Rachael Duncan, Nicola Hughes, Sophia Jones, Coleen Starkey, Kate Towers, Dee Babudoh, Adwoa Brown, Mimie Hollist, Mary Santo, Theresa Bailey, Ato Johnson, Liz Dungate and Tolu Odeneye.

To everyone who is reading this: know that you were created for awesome things and I hope this book helps you to believe that.

And to our Creator – thank you for choosing me.

Section One

Lessons from success

I looked at my mum and beamed; I'd got an A. She was pleased I got an A. I was a success. Fastforward a few years, and I was looking down at my university acceptance letter and feeling the same glow of pride warm me from the inside out; I was a success. It was only when the knocks started coming that I realized that what I had learnt from an early age about what it meant to be successful was entirely connected to what I had achieved in the world's eyes. And that, in turn, had become deeply connected with my sense of self-worth.

I know my upbringing is probably not that unique, but in a family striving for excellence (and very often hitting the mark), I have often felt like the outlier. The following section explores what it has meant to me to 'fail' and how I am learning to see success in the smallest things.

Success and failure go hand in hand; what is one without the relative experience of the other? And yet, we so often want to fastforward to the success stage. Even today it is hard to embrace what the world perceives as 'failure', but I am learning time and time again to look to what God thinks about me in these moments, turning to the Bible to explore God's often countercultural perspective on 'success'. I am still learning that God cares less about outward achievements and more about our inner world – the state of our hearts. I hope some of these thoughts help in unpacking and challenging the world's view of success and that they encourage us to see our failures and successes as God sees them: a way to draw ourselves and others closer to him.

LESSON 1

Live 'unsuccessfully'

Then I observed that most people are motivated to success because they envy their neighbours. But this, too, is meaningless – like chasing the wind.

—Ecclesiastes 4.4 (NLT)

Knowingly or not, many of us worship the idea of being successful. We want the awards, the recognition, the accolades. From a very early age, we start to develop our views on 'success'. Some may have been encouraged that it's the 'taking part that counts'. Others will have learned that we either win or lose, and to desperately avoid the latter. I come from a family of achievers; the only place to be in a race was first. This set me up for a feeling of inadequacy in any competition I did not win – not to mention for becoming a terrible loser. These days, people are so mindful of how we learn to define success at an early age that many schools have stopped having 'winners' and 'losers' to avoid upsetting the children (and, I presume, their parents). We not only learn how to 'win' and 'lose' – we also learn how we should react in either case. For many of us, we know what to do when we win: we celebrate. We champagne as if it's a verb. But what do we do when we fail? I bet most of us fall into one of two camps: depressed unto death or straight back onto the horse to try again. But what if success isn't all it's cracked up to be? And what if we've got it all wrong? In the Book of Ecclesiastes, King Solomon (undoubtedly successful by the world's standards) exposes how the motive to succeed is often one of comparison: 'because they envy their neighbours' and how the pursuit of this success is 'like chasing the wind'. I know

I can relate to this. Throughout my life I've fallen into the trap of setting myself new measures to be 'successful', and then, if and when I get there, the goal post seems to move: it's the *next* accolade that will make me truly successful. And the problem is, we can never get 'there'. Instead of seeing success as a destination, a win or lose, God's vision of 'success' is much more about who we are becoming rather than what we do. That's why the word 'unsuccessful' in the subtitle of this book is in quotation marks; what may look unsuccessful in the world's eyes is not unsuccessful to God. On my own journey to what I *thought* was success, I experienced what felt like so many 'nearlies', all of which made me feel a failure in those areas. But if we choose to see success through God's eyes, the whole story changes. All of my mistakes and near misses become lessons to learn from and areas for growth. For God is more interested in who I've been becoming when I *nearly* got into 'Britain's Next Top Model' (twice) to pursue my dream of being a catwalk model or when I *nearly* got my first graduate job at Christian Dior to begin a glittering career in luxe PR. Until recently, I have looked at these times as moments of failure. And in the world's eyes they are. However, with God, these times are not the end of the story – better a moment to embrace and learn from than forever 'chasing the wind'. The questions we need to ask ourselves in these moments are, what are we going to learn from this? And more importantly, what are we going to do now?

LESSON 2

Stories for success

Here is a trustworthy saying that deserves full acceptance: Christ Jesus came into the world to save sinners—of whom I am the worst. But for that very reason I was shown mercy so that in me, the worst of sinners, Christ Jesus might display his immense patience as an example for those who would believe in him and receive eternal life.

—1 Timothy 1.15–16 (NIV)

From my complicated family life and the untimely death of my daughter, to my unwanted divorce and struggles with sex, the reflections in this book detail some of the most intimate and so-called 'unsuccessful' parts of my life. Five or so years ago, in the aftermath of my divorce, a well-meaning friend told me not to worry: 'Just think of how you will be able to use your experiences to help others!' she said with a beaming smile. I smiled back and nodded because, well, I wasn't brought up to be rude, but I was seething. *Was that it?* I was doomed to a life of misery for the sole purpose of other people benefitting from all the crap I had gone through? It was also around that time that I started to read the words of the Apostle Paul, one of the most well-known figures in the Bible, in a new light. Paul wrote a large part of what we now know as the New Testament and was a powerful advocate for Jesus, but he was also once a powerful enemy to the believers at that time. His conversion is described in Acts Chapter 9: God speaks to a believer called Ananias and tells him that this persecutor is now on his side, 'for Saul is my chosen instrument to take my message to the Gentiles and to kings, as well as to the people of Israel.' Paul suffered a lot during his ministry, similar to the suffering he inflicted on the believers before his conversion, but his life and words have continued to be an example for people all over the world many years after his death. In the above scripture, a letter he wrote to an associate of his called Timothy, he says, 'But for that very reason I was shown mercy so that in me, the worst of sinners, Christ Jesus might display his immense patience as an example for those who would believe in him and receive eternal life.' Paul accepts the circumstances he has been called to, knowing that his purpose is bigger, and God will use all the aspects of his life – good and bad – to bring glory to God. I used to struggle with the idea that God would want me to go through so much pain, and I don't believe he does. God doesn't relish our unhappiness at all. The Bible says 'He hears our cries and that he collects our tears' (Ps. 56.8), but we live in an imperfect world of which pain and suffering play a part. When I think about my testimony and the people who tell me they felt free to talk about similar experiences or that they can identify with what I'm saying, I realize that God has called me to a purpose, a purpose in keeping with what life's journey has developed in me. If any of the reflections in this book help you in your journey or encourage you to share your own for the glory of God, I am teaching myself to join with Paul in praising God for how he chooses to use us to share his gift of life with others – and what could be a more 'successful' purpose in life than that?

LESSON 3

Let the music play

'Enjoy prosperity while you can,
but when hard times strike, realize that both come from God.
Remember that nothing is certain in this life.'
—Ecclesiastes 7.14 (NLT)

When it comes to music, I've always been a track-skipper. Since I got my first album, *Take That & Party*, at the age of eight, I've rarely (read, 'never') listened to a complete album one track after another. Instead I prefer to pick and choose my favourite songs and skip my way through, whether I'm listening at home, at work or on the go. In fact, even as recently as last weekend while driving home, I had finished playing my favourite tracks and was suddenly aware that I hardly knew any of the other songs on the album and was getting bored with my chosen few. It got me thinking that I can be the same way with seasons. When I've gone through tough times, I just want my life to speed up. Even though I've known in those times that no season lasts forever, I always just want to get to a better one *now*. I don't want to have to deal with the rest of the album, to go through the tracks that are not so great. I just want to skip to the good ones. I think so much of this season-skipping is tied up in how we see success. In the seasons where I am thriving, I'd be happy to replay them over and over again. It's the sticky, apparently 'unsuccessful' seasons that I want to skip. Once again, much wisdom is to be found in the musings of King Solomon in the Bible. In this quote from Ecclesiastes Chapter 7, he reminds us that both good times and hard times in life are inevitable and to 'remember that nothing is certain in this life.'

Far from depressing, this verse should remind us when hard times come that God isn't absent, and that he is always going to teach us something or grow us through these seasons. It also reminds us to enjoy the good times when they come. And though King Solomon reminds us that 'nothing in life' is certain, the Bible also tells us that 'Jesus Christ is the same yesterday, today and forever' (Heb. 13.8, NIV) and though seasons change, he will remain the same. I wish I could say that this realization made me want to stop and listen to the other tracks on the album, that maybe I would appreciate my favourite tracks more while mixed in with the rest. But to be honest, I still want to fast forward to the best bits, and it's still so often the same with my life. However, meditating on this verse does remind me that if I can't change where I am right now, I might as well listen to the track that's playing and see what God wants me to get out of it. I'll try to enjoy whatever new beat he is adding into the mix.

LESSON 4

30 before 30

I remember the deeds of the LORD;
yes, I will remember your wonders of old.

—Psalm 77.11 (NIV)

I went through a stressful period not long ago where I was trying to figure out what I wanted to do with my life. I had been in my job for almost a decade (I was promoted twice, okay? I wasn't just sitting there.) and was looking for my next adventure. But I had no idea what to do. All around me, people were focusing on bucket lists: 30 before 30 or 40 before 40. I read through other people's lists, and all they did was make me feel anxious about all the things I hadn't done yet. So I decided to create my own list, a list of things I had already achieved from school achievements through university and the workplace. In doing this, I realized just how much I had forgotten. Sometimes we can be so busy looking forward – chasing that ever-elusive 'success' – that we forget to thank God for what he has already done in us and through us. The psalmist in Psalm 77.11 cries, 'I remember the deeds of the Lord; yes, I will remember your wonders of old.' He calls us not only to trust him looking forward, but to use his faithfulness in the past to build our confidence in the brilliant things to come. As I looked back, I realized that things that once had me shrieking with joy were forgotten in the wake of comparison. This process of looking back reminded me of the many ways God has blessed me and the wonderful things I've been able to be a part of. And, if what we look back on is really hard, we can turn to the Bible to remind us of God's faithfulness to his people. Just like my list of things God has already done in my life, in the Bible we find list after list and record after record of what God has faithfully done in the lives of others, many of whom were well past doing a '30 before 30'.

LESSON 5

It takes two

Commit your actions to the Lord, and your plans will succeed.
—Proverbs 16.3 (NLT)

We often begin a new year with positive thinking about how we can improve our previous selves. Whether that means diet, exercise regime, work or relationship status (or all of the above), the changes we demand of ourselves are often drastic and with that, our good intentions are prone to quickly wane. It's such a common occurrence that most of us don't even pretend otherwise, but these kinds of fad commitments usually only benefit the sometimes unassuming investors in our inevitable fallout (steakhouses, wine bars and the ex we said we'd never go back to – and with good reason.) I love the simple but strong life lesson in this scripture: 'Commit your actions to the Lord, and your plans will succeed.' When I have read this in the past, I have misinterpreted it to mean, if we tell God our plans, they will succeed and what we have asked for will, to use an expression that seemingly only Christians use, 'come to pass'. But what does that look like in reality? God has been teaching me to look closely at the words used. I don't speak Greek or Hebrew so I wouldn't be able to decipher any of the original texts, but I frequently check synonyms to make sure I am reading it correctly. Synonyms for the word "commit" are pledge, devote, dedicate. The importance here is in the word 'action', defined in the Oxford dictionary as 'the process of doing something, typically to achieve an aim'. With this in mind, I see this scripture as a two-sided agreement in which we first do our part and then call upon God to engage him to do his. If we pledge a decision of our own making but then do nothing about it to follow-up, then we can't expect to get any kind of positive result (except of course, for God's grace). But when we follow through on the action we have decided on, we can dedicate it to God knowing that he listens to our prayers (Ps. 66.19) and that's what makes our plans 'succeed'. We all know that New Year's resolutions are hard to stick to, so to give ourselves a fighting chance, why not put a time limit on your life change? Decide to change your diet for two weeks, recording how you feel each day and then at the end, take stock and evaluate if it has any place in your future routine. Give yourself a taste of the life you think you want before you jump into it, knowing that the important thing is to commit wholeheartedly, calling on God's strength to help us 'succeed'.

LESSON 6

This face isn't going to sell itself

So God created human beings in his own image,
in the image of God he created them;
male and female he created them.

—Genesis 1.27 (NLT)

I've lost count of the number of times strangers have stopped me in the street to ask if I model. And I don't say that from a place of pride. I am almost six feet and believe me, I've not always been thankful for it – I didn't quite appreciate constantly being picked for the male role in school plays. Despite photographers often suggesting I just 'go for it', I never did manage to make it my full-time career. After a stint of auditioning for *Britain's Next Top Model,* I took to the streets in London and later New York to find representation at a more well-known agency. I received many, many 'no' responses, but each came with a recommendation to try another agency. I only discovered a potential reason why when a booker took the time to explain that these agencies didn't book many black models and so when they said 'try elsewhere', sometimes what they were really saying was 'we've reached our black quota' – usually, of one. This shocked me, reminding me again of the strength people need to thrive in an industry which can be both dismissive and fickle in its ideals of beauty. Thankfully, God has different ideas. This verse from Genesis reminds me that God created mankind in his own image: 'male and female he created them' and black and white and all the shades in between – he created them. Once again, God's idea of 'successful' beauty is wholly different from the world's. Once we fully understand this, we can push into opportunities with confidence – leaving it to God to decide whether the doors open or not. Free from the judgement of others, free from the damning fear of rejection, we also get to enjoy it more. I love modelling. And looking back, if I surrender this pursuit to God, I realize again that I've not been 'unsuccessful' but I've had loads of great experiences. I have modelled at London and Paris Fashion Weeks and enjoyed loads of different memories in that industry. I also try to look for God's will in this pursuit. I don't like to give excuses for God or reasons for why he allows things to happen or not, but I sometimes wonder what kind of lifestyle I would have lived as a full-time model. What would that have looked like in practice for someone so desperate to fit in and be liked and found worthy? The sense that my affirmation should come from outside of me is something I still struggle with today, and I can see how that would have been hugely amplified in such an industry. But perhaps seeking affirmation outside myself is not entirely wrong; it's just misdirected. Affirmation is to be found in who God says we are, and in seeking 'success', we need to remember to put his plans first.

LESSON 7

Learning to grow

We can make our plans,
but the LORD determines our steps.

—Proverbs 16.9 (NLT)

Not long after I turned 30, I applied to do a ski season in the French Alps. Having never skied before, it was a huge learning curve but also an amazing experience I will never forget. When I finally left the clean air of the Alps and came back to London to find my snot was black, I knew it was time to do something. I had heard that house-plants were good for purifying the air, so I decided to take some on – I promise, I wasn't turned by all the pictures of Kentia palms on Instagram. I picked a Peace Lily (which I called Annie) and a Zamioculcas zamiiflora (Annabelle) and put both in my bedroom along-side a new lamp from Zara Home. So far so pretty. I took the appropriate snaps for social media and waited for the health benefits to kick in. A few days later, I could have sworn there were insects flying around the room as I woke up feeling itchy. Annie's flowers started to brown, so I took her upstairs to our glass-covered exten-sion in case she just needed more sunlight. The next day, all her leaves had completely drooped. I tried watering her, not watering her and moved her to about four different positions in the room. I finally found one she liked: not too light, not too dark. She liked to be watered only when super thirsty and even then, it had to be luke-warm water served from the bottom up. What a drama queen! By contrast, Annabelle needed hardly any looking after, and I was super excited to see three buds popping out of the soil. That was eight months ago and those buds are now growing taller than the original branches. These two plants didn't do much to counter London's smog, but they did get me thinking. Sometimes, we can spend so much time and energy trying to make something work, when all the time, there is growth, but in somewhere we overlooked when our focus was elsewhere. There is so much to learn from the book of Proverbs, and this verse in Chapter 16 is one to hold in the forefront of our minds when we find ourselves trying too hard and not seeing the fruit in our lives: 'we can make our plans, but the Lord determines our steps.' It is so good to remember that, though we can fight to make something happen, God determines what will flourish and what will not. And when he does, when God starts to reveal what he has been doing in our lives, it will be so *there* and so obvious and so beautiful. And all we had to do was let him get on with it.

LESSON 8

Use your sword

A final word: Be strong in the Lord and in his mighty power. Put on all of God's armour so that you will be able to stand firm against all strategies of the devil. For we are not fighting against flesh-and-blood enemies, but against evil rulers and authorities of the unseen world, against mighty powers in this dark world, and against evil spirits in the heavenly places. Therefore, put on every piece of God's armour so you will be able to resist the enemy in the time of evil. Then after the battle you will still be standing firm. Stand your ground, putting on the belt of truth and the body armour of God's righteousness. For shoes, put on the peace that comes from the Good News so that you will be fully prepared. In addition to all of these, hold up the shield of faith to stop the fiery arrows of the devil. Put on salvation as your helmet, and take the sword of the Spirit, which is the word of God.

—Ephesians 6.10–17 (NLT)

Sometimes life can feel like a boxing ring. It can feel as though each time we overcome something, another issue comes up. I can literally imagine it – a huge heavyweight on one side, with bright red gloves, and me, petrified (although fashionably attired), on the other. Some days I feel like I'm doing a good job of bouncing around and avoiding the punches. But when those red gloves make contact, I am down. And I fall hard. Sometimes for a few seconds, sometimes for much longer. But when I came across this scripture in Ephesians 6, I realized that while I had deflected some 'attacks' with the faith I have in

God, I wasn't actually fighting back. I was only using one part of the armour we have been given. This scripture reminds us that we have been given tools to fight against the spiritual battles we face and not just a shield to deflect it. The attacks we face can come in the form of negative emotions and difficult situations, and my mistake was not addressing them with the right 'weapons'. I was trusting that God would work all things for my good (Romans 8.28), but I wasn't using anything else to push forward in what often felt like an ongoing battle. I wasn't fighting against failure; I was just metaphorically crossing my fingers and hoping for the best. I have memorized this scripture to remind me of the weaponry God has given us to cope with difficult situations, and one of the things I wasn't using was my 'sword', the word of God in the Bible. I wasn't speaking God's precious words over my life and letting them encourage me to push through uncertainty with confidence and assurance. It has struck me that when I do this, I can get through difficult situations with less stress and less frustration. Okay, so sometimes there are moments where all we can do is stand firm, and that's fine. But this scripture shows us that we are also called to get up and fight for a victorious finish in our battle for faith. Whatever you are going through today, whatever lies are clouding your mind and stopping you from seeing that the war against the enemy is already won, I pray that you would open God's Word and find a scripture that slices through the lie, fighting for the truth.

LESSON 9

Stay in your lane

He renews my strength.
He guides me along right paths,
  bringing honor to his name.

—Psalm 23.3 (NLT)

At school I ran 100m sprint, 100m hurdles and the last leg in relay. Standing alongside girls from the other houses, I could see the same length of track stretching in front of us and the same obstacles to overcome. All I needed to beat my opponents was speed, and speed I did. This mirrored my life at the time. At school, my classmates and I were going through the system together – studying the same syllabus and being given the same homework and the same tests. It was only when I reached adulthood that I started to notice the differences between our runs. Suddenly, we were on separate life journeys, progressing at varying paces, and no matter how fast I tried to run, it felt like I could never quite catch up. Reading this scripture in Psalms, I was reminded that God is guiding me along my own unique path and that only by embracing my own hurdles and oppositions would it bring honour to his name. I've a tendency to take on life's hiccups as my own personal failure without recognizing that we live in a world where things do go wrong and, more importantly, that God knows a way to guide us that will bring us through and show that he is good. The success of our journeys isn't for anyone else to experience. We will never do or feel things in quite the same way as our friends, and like it or not, that's exactly how God intended it to be. While I know I have some questions for God when my time on earth is up, we'll have the benefit of hindsight to help us see what we couldn't see at the time. Maybe the journey we took has equipped us to thrive where we are now or maybe we'll never know why it happened. But we can take comfort in the knowledge that trusting God to guide us means we don't have to understand it all.

LESSON 10
Don't believe the hype

It is better to be godly and have little
    than to be evil and rich.
For the strength of the wicked will be shattered,
    But the Lord takes care of the godly.

—Psalm 37.16–17 (NLT)

We live in a world increasingly obsessed with goals and status, and so it can be tempting to use other people as a gauge to how well we are doing, looking to their public success indicators to direct our own. Everything is online, inviting even more competition, and there is always someone already doing what you are doing or wanting to do. When they seem to be smashing ceilings you didn't even know existed, it can put you off from even starting. I spent many years thinking that other people were stealing my ideas before someone finally told me two important things. First, if someone else is doing something similar and it is successful, that shows there's a market for it. And second, it's not really my idea unless I do something with it. Whether you want to write a book, become Prime Minister, break a world record or run your own business, don't forget that your invisible (or not) Wikipedia page recounts the journey, not just the destination. Chapter 37 in Psalms is effectively advising us not to look at what other people are doing. The first two words are comfortingly familiar: 'Don't worry', and while primarily talking about not envying the lives of people who do not honour God, it definitely applies when it comes to the way in which we can envy peoples' lives from afar, without having the faintest idea about what they are involved in

21

or how they live their lives. And regardless of what someone else is doing or not doing, God is primarily concerned with the way you live your life, not what you're seemingly getting out of it. You are the sum of your parts which includes everything you have experienced and learned on your everyday journey. So, while you may still be working towards something, if you are following God in your life, let me tell you, you are successful right now.

Section Two

Lessons from work

'What do you want to be when you grow up?' was never a question I struggled to answer when I was young. I was going to be a model and a journalist. Not necessarily in that order and not necessarily at the same time, but yep, I was definitely going for that MoJo life. I felt sorry for my friends and classmates who shrugged their shoulders at the same question, and so it was a shock when my career path took some far from linear turns.

It has taken years to realize how much I had hinged my sense of purpose on this very specific career plan coming to fruition. I know I'm probably not alone in feeling like growing up sometimes feels like a bit of a scam, and mustering up the energy to get out of bed on Monday morning is the epitome of adulthood. 'Is this life?' I would often ask myself. At work, we navigate pay rises, difficult colleagues and the doubt we sometimes feel about whether we are even qualified to do our jobs. It's a whole mood, and not always a happy one. On the other hand, some of us can become obsessed with living to work, our ambition knowing no ends.

God has had to remind me repeatedly that balance is key; we have to balance the energy we get from work with rest and play. He also teaches us to believe that the one who gave us the gifts we use in work doesn't waste any opportunity for us to learn in every situation. I hope these findings I've stumbled through will invite you to reflect on your God-given purpose both in and outside of work.

LESSON 11

The lie of 'Mondays'

So the creation of the heavens and the earth and everything in them was completed. On the seventh day God had finished his work of creation, so he rested from all his work. And God blessed the seventh day and declared it holy, because it was the day when he rested from all his creation.

—Genesis 2.1–3 (NLT)

Like many of us, I couldn't wait to leave school and start working. The ability to earn my own money and be my own boss was the life I longed for, especially following my first taste of journalism at 16 on a two-week internship with a women's magazine. It was incredible, and I loved everything about it, even down to my zone five to zone one commute — a novelty at the time. I've worked in many different roles since — some good and some not so — but the message we keep hearing is that we should all expect to dread Mondays. We spend most of our waking hours in some kind of work capacity, and yet many have adopted an accepted attitude of 'hate work, love play' so often displayed across social media. At the risk of sounding like the Fri-yay party pooper, I don't think God has created us to live like this. In Genesis, we read that God himself worked for six days and then rested on the seventh. It might not look like a fair balance for those of us campaigning for a three-day weekend, but the Bible does say that he was pleased with what he had created and that 'God saw that it was good' (Gen. 1.10b). Maybe that's what we're missing out on? The ability to recognize that work was always part of God's plan, and that work can be good. Most of my working life thus far has been spent on magazines, a deadline-driven industry that means I'm usually focused on the publication date. Everything that comes before that is simply part of a long 'to do' list I have to get through before I reach the end. Chasing people for content is tedious, and having to rewrite articles over and over again can feel soul-destroying, but it took me some time before I fully realized the importance of every cog in the wheel of what I do. Every bit is important to its conclusion, which means I should be recognizing my achievements every day – just like God did. This account of creation in Genesis reminds us afresh that work and rest were always part of God's Plan A. He didn't intend work to be a roadblock to how we were truly meant to spend our time. You may enjoy the weekends more than the weekdays, but the Bible consistently reminds us to not live our lives waiting for something better to happen while failing to recognize God's blessings for us right now.

LESSON 12

Lessons from younger you

Direct your children onto the right path,
and when they are older, they will not leave it.

—Proverbs 22.6 (NLT)

In a seminar by The School of Life entitled 'A Job to Love', it was suggested that in order to find out what truly makes us tick, we should try to remember what we loved doing as children. What were the things we sought out to do, that no one had to force on us, that we would happily spend hours indulging in? Sometimes these habits remain until our early and even late teens, but when we start to consider the work environment and stable career choices, those hobbies can often take a back seat. It is ironic, then, that when we come to a stage further on in our lives, it is suggested that we return to the thing we once abandoned for money, security or ambition. It's interesting that in the biblical texts, children are counted as 'other' (as are women), with the numbers recorded within its pages usually representing men alone. And yet, the words Jesus himself speaks are of how important our little people are (Matt. 19.13–14; Mark 10.13–16; Luke 18.15–17; Matt. 18.2–5). While it is right to think that wisdom usually comes with experience, this scripture in Proverbs speaks to me of the call from God that we recognize in our often uncomplicated, simplistic childhood minds – and then leave later on because it seems too hard or improbable. Sometimes, people pursuing their dreams can be accused of being childish or selfish. 'Grow up!' we might say to the person who dreams of being a pilot but is currently working in a telesales job. We might mean well, but is that fair? The reason I went to this seminar was because I went through a stage of people asking me, 'if you could do anything in the world, what would you do?' And I didn't have a clue. Me, who had always been so sure of myself and my future. My uncle, with whom I spent a lot of time when I was a teenager, told me I had huge plans back then – 'you wanted to take over the world!' So in a bid to try and get back that passion for life and purpose, I tried to imagine what a younger version of me would be saying to the person I am today. What would she think about what I had achieved so far? Would she see it as having gone off course? Not quite where we wanted to be? And was there something else I had forgotten about? I wonder how you'd answer the same questions. In taking a trip down my own memory lane, it amused me to remember how fearless I was. I would do anything, and did, on lots of occasions. In looking back, I remembered some positive feedback I received from a panel interview stating, 'Is there anything this girl can't do?' And as I trust God to guide me, I'm encouraged to find out.

LESSON 13

Imposter syndrome

We are confident of all this because of our great trust in God through Christ. It is not that we think we are qualified to do anything on our own. Our qualification comes from God.

—2 Corinthians 3.4–5 (NLT)

When I was younger, I was determined: I knew who I was and where I wanted to be. As I've gotten older, however, I have often found myself wondering if I am really good enough for the job? Who was this person who was trusted to do all this work? To sign off magazines and edit Board-level documents? I started to doubt myself and would wait with bated breath each time I signed off a budget, dreading the arrival of an email asking me *what the hell I'd been doing* or telling me how rubbish my work was. It was only when I started to spend time with people outside of my industry that I realized that I actually *was* equipped to do my job. The problem was, I was assessing my ability against the people around me. This verse from Corinthians 3. 4–5 exposes the problem: 'it is not that we think we are qualified to do anything on our own.' I was so busy looking to other people to qualify me and validate me that I let comparison unsettle the root of my identity. Instead, this verse reminds us that 'our qualification comes from God.' Even though we may need certain qualifications to take on a role, this should be separate from our identity. Our identity is secure in God and who he says we are. It is from this place that we can approach the tasks he has for us to do with confidence. When you find yourself drawn to comparison and self-doubt, it is good to remember that it is God who qualifies and not to take the gifts he has given you for granted. Just because you do what you do every day and think nothing of it, doesn't mean you don't do a pretty good job. You are good enough, your identity is qualified.

LESSON 14

Attitude is everything

For the despondent, every day brings trouble;
for the happy heart, life is a continual feast.

—Proverbs 15.15 (NLT)

No one wants to be unhappy. We spend most of our lives seeking ways to make ourselves feel happier, whether that's with material things or trying to ease our emotions through alcohol or Netflix addictions. A happy heart as mentioned in the above scripture can seem screamingly elusive, perhaps particularly in the context of working life. Like me, my friend Laura dislikes mess, being cold and people who are inconsiderate. Unlike with me, you wouldn't know that if you spoke with her in any of these situations. Laura's personal mantra is to always try and make the best of things and so, accosted by any of the above, she remains polite, gracious and unruffled. I get that as a concept and have read many times that it's not *what* happens but how you *respond* to it that matters. I knew all that and agreed, but it wasn't until my life ran into a kind of Groundhog Day that the words of this scripture really got under my skin. I found myself sick of feeling low and disenchanted with my work and was tired of hearing myself complain about the same things – especially those things that weren't subject to any immediate change: my commute, my flatmates, some of my colleagues – so I made a conscious decision to do the opposite of whatever my default negative reaction was in these areas. These verses show us that when we are low in spirit – though often justified through illness, sickness or disappointment – we can increase our wellbeing and ensure better days when our focus is on

Jesus. Many podcasts and self-help books would tell us to retain a positive attitude – and there's a lot of truth in that. But for us as Christians, we don't need to muster up good vibes; we can remind ourselves of the source of our joy, Jesus. He in turn has the power to shift our perspective dramatically – but we need to be open to let him. I really wanted to put this scripture to the test, so in order to project a happy heart, I started spending more time with God and his word. The results were clear to see: I began being a lot more accommodating at work, saying 'yes' when I really wanted to say 'no'. I tried to be kind on public transport, saying 'thank you' to the driver and letting people go in front of me on the tube. I also made a point of spending time with my flatmates when I got home – it turned out we had a lot more in common than I thought. After about a week, I felt calmer and less stressed out even though outwardly, nothing had changed. When a friend who hadn't seen me in a while came to visit, she said, 'you've changed.' But I hadn't, not really. I just stopped letting situations change me.

LESSON 15

You don't have to be a 'girl boss'

Better to have little, with godliness,
than to be rich and dishonest.

—Proverbs 16.8 (NLT)

I have a quote-based Pinterest board so there's no way I could have missed the many, *many* posts encouraging me to be a 'girl boss' alongside advice on how to 'slay' ('Throw your hair into a bun and handle it!') and to be honest, it's getting boring. I was a '90s teen, brought up in the Spice Girls, Girl Power era. We had TLC and Destiny's Child encouraging us to be strong, powerful and independent women. And we are. Then the marketing mogul that is social media came along and tried to make us into clones of each other with visual representations of the ideal strong, independent woman for us to replicate: a woman who runs her own business, goes to the gym five times a week, spends Sunday evening doing meal prep for her whole family, is always perfectly put together and has super cute, talented children. We all know that what we see online can often be very different IRL, but the rise of influencers suggests we are still hooked on this 'ideal'. I love the book of Proverbs for providing practical wisdom that still speaks into our 21st century lives. This is one of several passages decrying an obsession with 'riches'. In saying 'Better to have little, with godliness than to be rich and dishonest,' this proverb speaks loudly into whom we choose to follow and/or imitate. It's always good to evaluate your emotions after spending any length of time on social media to see how they are affecting this motive. For me, I realized that an extended perusal of these accounts left me feeling exhausted and less than – craving the 'riches' of others rather than being thankful for the 'little' I had. It's great if that really *is* your life, but for those who are striving towards this ideal, it is important to check our hearts: are we trying to be or portray ourselves as a 'girl boss' to be liked and found worthy? Or do we know that in Jesus we are already enough? What's more, some people like being able to go home at 5 p.m. without any overheads to worry about at night, or for walking to be their chosen form of exercise. Not everyone wants to be a boss and that's okay. God is searching to see whether we are aligning our lives with his will, and that looks different for all of us.

LESSON 16

Learning humility

Then Jesus and his disciples left Jerusalem and went into the Judean countryside. Jesus spent some time with them there, baptizing people. At this time John the Baptist was baptizing at Aenon, near Salim, because there was plenty of water there; and people kept coming to him for baptism. [24] (This was before John was thrown into prison.) A debate broke out between John's disciples and a certain Jew over ceremonial cleansing. So John's disciples came to him and said, 'Rabbi, the man you met on the other side of the Jordan River, the one you identified as the Messiah, is also baptizing people. And everybody is going to him instead of coming to us.' John replied, 'No one can receive anything unless God gives it from heaven. You yourselves know how plainly I told you, "I am not the Messiah. I am only here to prepare the way for him." It is the bridegroom who marries the bride, and the bridegroom's friend is simply glad to stand with him and hear his vows. Therefore, I am filled with joy at his success. He must become greater and greater, and I must become less and less.'

—John 3.22–30 (NLT)

Last year was the hardest in my career. Effectively demoted in my role and given a new line manager who, quite frankly, I felt was way out of his depth, I wore my disdain like a cloak, flinging it over my shoulders with every dramatic exit from a meeting. I can't tell you how much I wanted out of that job. I was applying for what felt like everything and anything, but nothing was working out. Everyone around me seemed to be flourishing, both my fellow team members and friends outside of work, and I started to panic. I had always been a ringleader in my friendship groups, and now it seemed as though I was being left behind. I had every Christian I knew praying for me and every creative looking out for new roles. Then one morning when I was praying about it, I came to a page in my devotional which talked about how, while God wants us to thrive in our workplaces, he is primarily interested in how our work situation is developing our character. I struggle with the thinking that God allows the negative things that happen in our lives, especially when his character is kind and good, but what I realize is that God works through taxing situations to bring about positive change to the core of who we are and how we operate in the world. This scripture draws out that character trait that feels so at odds with much of the world, who are taught to seek seniority and high levels of authority: humility. John the Baptist was great in his own right, but even he recognized that he was only a precursor to someone even greater: 'he must become greater and greater and I must become less and less.' John the Baptist understood his identity in relationship to Jesus. His standing in relation to the Son of God did not diminish him in a negative way; it freed him to enjoy more of the goodness of God. And as I read that, I remembered asking God to help me learn about humility. I knew I had a tendency to be proud (a classic Nigerian trait), and it had started to bother me. It's certainly not what I wanted, but I guess there's no other way to learn humility than to be humbled. From then on, I made a conscious decision to stop complaining about things and to basically just do what I was told. I stopped questioning things, stopped pointing out what I saw as other people's incompetence and just got on with it. I told my team to do the same and soon, the office even felt lighter. I left any work issues at work and shut down the kind of bitchy talk I would previously have initiated. Looking back, I realize what a nightmare I must have been to manage. The writer C. S. Lewis said that 'true humility is not thinking less of yourself; it's thinking of yourself less,' and it was through this hard season that God began to teach me about what it means to be humble. Well, I did ask.

LESSON 17

Trust him

Trust in the Lord with all your heart; do not depend on your own understanding. Seek his will in all you do, and he will show you which path to take.

—Proverbs 3.5–6 (NLT)

At the end of the year, I decided that my word for the next would be 'trust'. And, to be honest, I feel like God took me way too seriously. I was encouraged by my friend Oyinda, who has been choosing a word for each year pretty much as long as I've known her, selecting words like hope and faith to remind her daily life of their power and her purpose. As a writer, words are particularly important to me, so I was reluctant to limit myself to just one for a whole 365 days – but given the rocky year I was coming out of, I felt it was important to name the season I was heading into: *trust.* As I explored the scriptures, it was my glimpses into the lives of past believers – Noah, Esther, Joseph – that showed me that those who get the most out of a relationship with God are the ones who trust him completely. Added to this, another scripture from Proverbs sprang to mind: 'Trust the Lord with all your heart…Seek his will in all you do, and he will show you which path to take.' And so, with this powerful scripture in my head and heart, I followed what I felt God leading me to do: resign from a stable full-time job to go freelance and work on my book. I didn't have a 'safety net' or a partner to support me, but the uncertainty and fear that might have accompanied my decision otherwise were not there. Some might call my decision stupid or reckless, and both words have crossed my mind. But then, there is this daring side that I think God puts in each of us that causes us to question the apparently 'safe' wisdom of the world. What if this turns out to be the best thing I have ever done? What if the crazy leap into the unknown that you are considering propels you into something incredible? All we have to do is trust in him and take the first step.

LESSON 18

Seeking perfection

Charm is deceptive and beauty is fleeting but a woman who fears the Lord is to be praised.

—Proverbs 31.30 (NIV)

I'd love to say the bias towards beauty I felt in the modelling industry has never spilled out into the less image conscious spaces in which I've worked. And yet, the older I get, the more I worry about my looks. I can no longer get away with bingeing on pepperoni pizza without my face projecting its likeness the next day. I know deep down that my desirability as an employee is not determined by my open pore count, but it doesn't stop me panicking about blemishes or when my boobs don't seem to sit as high as they used to. Christian or not, how can we possibly be immune to the images around us that sell us what seems to be a standardized reasoning for what makes us attractive to someone – both in and outside the workplace? Whispers on Twitter tell of organizations where women are hired based on their levels of attractiveness and turned away due to their being the 'wrong' race. It seems we are always trying to fit in, trying to tick all the boxes and make the grade – whatever that is. If there is a way to be a perfect woman, I'm pretty sure I've not mastered it. Proverbs is full of practical instructions for successful living, and the woman described between verses ten and 27 in this chapter is Mary Poppins-perfect in every way. She works both in and out of the house, gets up early, goes to bed late – once all her work is done, obviously. She cooks for the whole household, she sews, she always looks amazing, she has a great laugh, she's wise, she's kind, she's the perfect balance of strict and tender. To be honest, I find her exhausting in her awesomeness. But of course, the last 20 or so verses regularly get quoted to us women as the pinnacle for success. I've often interpreted Proverbs 31.30 – 'Charm is deceptive and beauty is fleeting but a woman who fears the Lord is to be praised' – as an admonishment. We are supposed to eschew focus on outward beauty and make sure we tick off 'perfect' using this list instead. Recently, I have understood it differently. The woman described was not someone who did all that and, as a result, was a 'Woman of God'. She was like that because her first love was God, and she feared him as she should. I'm guilty of trying to make myself likeable and attractive using some of the attributes of the Proverbs 31 woman. But when we love like God, give like God, help like God and give grace like God – that's what causes us to be attractive. Not that we should forget about what makes us physically well or generally likeable, but we should do it in God's way, spending time with him and growing in his likeness, a likeness that we see from the Bible is irresistibly attractive.

LESSON 19

Connect, create, collaborate

Two people are better off than one, for they can help each other succeed.

—Ecclesiastes 4.9 (NLT)

Between bloggers, influencers, reality TV stars and overnight celebrities, everyone seems to be starting something that is going to be the 'next big thing'. I'm all for harnessing creativity and starting new conversations, but I've also seen a lot of social accounts open with a flurry and then lie dormant as the enthusiasm wanes or the competition looks too hard – including, I hasten to add, my own. A couple of years ago I started working on a new idea prompted by a suggestion from a friend. I absolutely love lingerie and truly believe that when we have the right style and fit, it can be that hidden gem that gives us confidence from underneath – it doesn't need to be for anyone else to make you feel great. I was often asked for advice and shopping tips on what my friends should buy, and so the idea of turning this into a business seemed to make sense. I spent ages on the name, the wording for the website and nabbing all the relevant social handles, but I don't have the longest attention span, so you can guess how this venture ended – as quickly as it began. I still love lingerie and sometimes wonder whether I gave up on this venture prematurely, but what I do know is that it probably didn't help that I was trying to make it happen by myself. In my home of London, while we live closer to each other than ever, our sense of togetherness has been somewhat lost in a culture pursuing the singular aim of achieving, often wanting to say we did it alone. This scripture in Ecclesiastes reminds us that

God made us for community, saying 'two people are better off than one'. Though we are all 'fearfully and wonderfully made' (Ps. 139) to be perfectly unique, he made us all and we are all part of his family, each with different strengths and abilities. This very small sentence teaches us that we were designed to work together and when we do, we can both succeed. Even the fact that each of us was created by two people backs up this thinking that we were built for togetherness and when we collaborate, new life can happen – whether that's a baby or a project or a new venture. If you have an idea, why not put the feelers out among your friends and see who else would be interested in working together? Starting a new company can be exhausting, and it definitely helps to have someone with whom to share not only the 'burden', but also the common goal so that you can encourage each other on days when it all gets a bit too much. Or if you know any others who are already starting something, why not go and ask them if they could use some of your skills? Or do a skills swap – maybe you can write their copy if they can build your website? We weren't created to exist alone, so if you do nothing else, go find someone to connect with today.

LESSON 20

Our colleagues don't have to be our friends

Getting wisdom is the wisest thing you can do!
And whatever else you do, develop good judgment.
—Proverbs 4.7 (NLT)

One of my friends makes a point of never staying longer than two years in any organization. I'm the opposite, with two years being possibly the shortest length of time spent in any one company. If you're moving to a new workplace every few years, then I completely understand the reluctance to see every desk associate as a new BFF. For others, myself included, staying put can mean deep relationships can develop with the people you work with – we spend so much time with each other, after all. The balance between being work colleagues and friends can be a hard one to navigate, and for me personally, I've been guilty of overstepping those boundaries. I went through a rough period at work, and as my colleagues supported me, we found ourselves spending more time together, going for after-work drinks and eventually hanging out outside of the office. It took a dramatic fallout for me to realize the pressure I had placed on the 'colleague as friend' relationship. For some aspects of life and love, the Bible has clear-cut guidance; for many other scenarios, what will work well in some situations or be right for some people will not be appropriate at other times and for other people. This scripture in Proverbs is just one of many inviting us to seek wisdom and develop good judgement to help us discern the right way to navigate these grey-area situations. Though for some, work friends can be best friends, God helped me realize I was expecting my colleagues to fulfil the much bigger shoes of deeper friendship. He reminded me that when he created Adam, he surrounded him with lots of creature companions but none were right for the type of unity Adam needed. God reminded me that instead of trying to force-fit relationships to fulfil a certain need in us, we can trust him to provide everything we need. Once I shifted my focus to realize that not every relationship has to meet every need in us, I realized that there really is nothing wrong with seeing the workplace as somewhere to work, as opposed to an extension of your social life. With God's wisdom, I could see for me that my personal life and work life would benefit from a clear distinction, and that our colleagues definitely don't have to be our friends.

Section Three

Lessons from friendship

I had always found it easy to make friends. I joined clubs to find likeminded souls and poured endless energy and effort into those friendships. The problems came when I realized I expected the same in return and didn't receive it.

My Judy Blume books were full of BFFs and lifelong friendships, and I often struggled with the inevitable fallouts or when someone simply walked away. Spending time with God, away from WhatsApp groups, resulted in me realizing just how much time and energy I was demanding of my friends. I was expecting each one to satisfy all my emotional needs, which is unrealistic and unfair. Sadly, I think I lost a few friends that way. God showed me that only he can truly fulfil all our emotional needs, and he is here for that, always.

Over time, God has also helped me see that some friendships will just come to a natural end, and that's all right. One of my love languages is gifts, and so I have learned to focus on the joy I have in giving gifts rather than receiving them, since that's one thing within my control. I have learned to forgive friends who have hurt me and ask forgiveness of those who have been hurt by me. Our friends are usually the first significant relationships we form outside of our families, so as you read this, my hope is that you can look back on your own friendships and the lessons they have taught you, both those meant for a time and those built for a lifetime.

LESSON 21

Love lists

Love each other with genuine affection, and take delight in honouring each other.

—Romans 12.10 (NLT)

A love list is something I apparently coined and started in my oldest friendship group. In a group chat during our early twenties, one of my besties was bemoaning her well-paid but boring job as she started to doubt whether she would ever reach the very real goals she had for her dream career. At the time, my positivity knew no bounds (I was probably in the middle of my cycle), and I immediately went on the charm offensive to make her see how lucky she was. But she wasn't having it. Nothing I, or any of our other friends, could say was helping. So I started typing a list of her best qualities and told her exactly why I thought she was amazing. I honestly can't remember what I wrote, but apparently, she saved and kept it. It can be hard for us to see the positives in difficult or frustrating situations, and I have also experienced that weird kind of blindness when it comes to being able to recognize our own qualities against a sea of everyone else's. The Apostle Paul, author of Romans, dedicates Chapter 12 to instructions on how we can be living sacrifices to God. Chapter 2 reads, 'Don't copy the behaviour and customs of this world, but let God transform you into a new person by changing the way you think. Then you will learn to know God's will for you, which is good and pleasing and perfect.' Though God has the power to change the way we view ourselves, the verses above encourage us to 'love each other with genuine affection and take delight in honouring each other'.

Clearly, we too can have an impact on how our friends start to see themselves. When we make a point of showing honour to our friends, it puts us in a position of humility – thinking of ourselves less – which is pleasing to God. Sometime later, I was having a similar conversation with the same friendship group, but this time, it was me doing the lamenting. When my violins started playing, my friend told me to hold on and reappeared after a few minutes with her own list, this time for me. Even though my immediate situation did not change, I cannot tell you how much it meant to read those words of love and affirmation from someone who also knows my faults, bad habits and inadequacies. It doesn't even have to be that deep. One of my favourites was 'You always find free parties to go to – and that's a life skill.' Regardless of its impact, when we show love to our friends with genuine affection, we know it's a sacrifice pleasing to our almighty God. So, if you're feeling good today, write a love list for someone who might really need it.

LESSON 22

Do as I say, not as I do

If you need wisdom, ask our generous God, and he will give it
to you. He will not rebuke you for asking.

—James 1.5 (NLT)

We all have friends who are particularly quick to give their opinions.
I've been guilty of this on more than one occasion, and if I'm honest, too often our advice is provided from a perceived higher moral
position, usually backed up with Christian doctrine. Submitting
ourselves and our decision-making to this kind of inspection can
leave us feeling justified with the decision we finally make. We have
checked with those 'in the know' and as a result feel the outcome
has been well considered. But I've often found that when you fast
forward a few days, weeks, months or even years, many find themselves in a situation where those friends who had all the advice find
themselves in the same position and are not exactly practising what
they preached. I was in this situation around six years ago when,
following my divorce, I was missing the intimate connection sex
brings and was speaking openly about it with a Christian friend. She
assured me that sex was a marriage-based activity, and anything outside of that was not God's will for us, with Hebrews 13.4, of course,
reading, 'Marriage should be honoured by all, and the marriage bed
kept pure.' But the reason I was struggling with the issue in the first
place came from much deeper yearnings and frustrations I failed to
thrash out with God, and I instead deferred to my friend's advice. A
few months after our conversation, my friend called to tell me she
was pregnant, with someone she had met a few months earlier on

an online dating site. I congratulated her and chose not to bring up our conversation, but I did feel a bit cheated. I soon realized that it wasn't her fault; it was mine, for not taking responsibility for my own decisions and getting to the root of the wrestle with God. This scripture in James shows that we can always go and ask God for answers. He knows our struggles and 'will not rebuke [us] for asking'. Advice from friends is great but when we put the sole responsibility on them, it can prevent us from going right to the source. God wants us to have deep and direct relationship with him, so it's important to make sure we're always asking him to show us the way – not just our well-meaning friends. This way, when we make decisions, they are ones made *with* him and *for* him, bringing us in line with his plans for us.

LESSON 23

When their happy is too loud

Be happy with those who are happy, and weep with those who weep.

—Romans 12.15 (NLT)

I read a book recently in which the main character was advised by her mentor to celebrate every engagement, wedding, new birth or new job that her friends presented her with. It sounds pretty obvious, but I've learned that it's an important thing to remember as we journey together but at different speeds. While I generally like any excuse to pop a cork, sometimes the flurry of positive activity in the lives of my nearest and dearest can seem particularly overwhelming – especially alongside the absence of my own. Now if you're reading this having recently celebrated something amazing, and you can't understand why people just can't be happy for you regardless of their situation, please know that we *are* on your side. But feel free to turn over to another page and come back to this lesson at another time when you might understand a little better what I mean. The very nature of friendship combined with our individual personalities means there will be times when we clash and, having made different life choices, the outcomes and timings of big life events will vary from one to another. The exhortation here in Romans is for us to meet our friends at the point of connection with them rather than responding from a place of where we are. I am so appreciative of friends who have been sensitive to my grieving at a point where they have been celebrating, and one of my friends cried with relief when she realized that I was overjoyed at her baby news. It wasn't easy for me to lift my head up from the rubble of baby loss, and it would have been hard for her to know how to both celebrate and be supportive to my grief, but this is what true friendship is all about – God's will for us to love our neighbours as ourselves ('Do not seek revenge or bear a grudge against a fellow Israelite, but love your neighbour as yourself. I am the Lord.' – Lev. 19.18). I was one of the first in my group to get engaged, and there was an almost imperceptible feeling of jealousy among my friends. As life would have it, I'm now divorced and they're the ones getting married. We have to remember that life isn't linear. And like the mentor in my book advised, the best we can do is focus on celebrating each other at every opportunity. After all, real joy is contagious and champagne is for everyone (well, except pregnant women – please alcohol responsibly).

LESSON 24

Choose your audience

Don't look out only for your own interests, but take an interest in others, too.

—Philippians 2.4 (NLT)

Sometimes I feel like women are our own worst enemies. We complain about the way men have treated us, and yet we are still learning how to lift each other up. This might seem at odds with a lot of the current talk and books released on sisterhood, but if you take a cross section of conversations on social media, we are still so divided. I came off Facebook a few years ago because I found some of those conversations too draining, and one of those was about parenthood. Whatever social platform you're on (if any), you can't have failed to notice that there is a lot of 'women vs. women' one-upmanship taking place in this area. There's breastfeeding vs. bottle feeding, children vs. no children, single child vs. multiples. As for many, there is often not a lot of choice in most, if not all, of the above life situations; it seems a pretty pointless engagement. Posts like 'I don't understand how people without children can say they're tired', 'You've only got one child, try dealing with twins' or 'What's the point in having a baby if you can't even be bothered to feed it properly' really get to me. They're unhelpful and extremely insensitive. As Christians, we serve a God who reminds us that we should be outwardly focused and not seek to prove ourselves right or better than others. The earlier part of this scripture reads, 'Don't be selfish; don't try to impress others. Be humble, thinking of others as better than yourselves. Don't look out for only your own interests, but take an interest in others, too.' (Phil. 2.3–4) Not having living children of my own, I can't say I know what it's like to be woken by a crying baby ten times a night, but I can remember when I would have done anything to be in that position. So while I may not be physically shattered from sleep deprivation, I know I have been emotionally exhausted from that loss. I have friends who have really struggled with breastfeeding and feel like such failures when accosted by the "breast is best" brigade. As women, we have to deal with periods, hormones, glass ceilings, waxing, inequality, bad haircuts that take ages to grow out, the menopause, crappy side effects from the contraceptive pill, and so on. We have enough to deal with without needing to draw pointless battle lines. I'm not for one second suggesting that parents shouldn't be allowed to discuss these things, and there are plenty of helpful forums on- and offline where those things can be shared and debated. We all need to find a safe space to get the support we need, but before we rant about our situations, Paul calls us to 'take an interest in others too', to look out for others and choose our audiences accordingly.

LESSON 25

Here for a reason

If you keep quiet at a time like this, deliverance and relief for the Jews will arise from some other place, but you and your relatives will die. Who knows if perhaps you were made queen for just such a time as this?

—Esther 4.14 (NLT)

Even after more than thirty years on this planet, I'm always startled by the way God interweaves the plans he has for our lives with the lives of others. When I was moving out of my flat, I wasn't at all worried about finding someone to replace me. Everyone always said how lucky I had been to find it in the first place, and with so many renters in London, I felt quite smug to be in such a good position when I wanted to terminate my contract early. Everyone who came to see the room wanted it, but that's when the issues started. The first person we offered it to pulled out at the last minute, starting a ripple effect, and then we started having issues with the agency. I was running out of time and started to panic, thinking that maybe this was a sign that I shouldn't go ahead with the move even though I had found an amazing new home. I was very close to pulling out and urgently called a friend to pray with me. Before we began, she said simply, 'What if this isn't about you? What if these people just aren't right for the flat?' Too often our worlds can revolve around us, and it might not even occur to us that the things unfolding could be to line up things for someone else, not just ourselves. In the story of Esther, she had been picked over all the other single girls taken to be a part of the king's harem and had been appointed queen. But when her uncle

Mordecai asked her to take a petition to the king, she was afraid. No one was admitted to the king's presence without being invited, and although she was queen, Esther was under the same rules as everyone else. The last queen had been demoted for disobeying the king's order to come to him, but the punishment for uninvited entry was death. Esther was a woman and a Jew, in a household where neither was particularly respected. She had so far kept her background and nationality a secret, and this would mean explaining who she really was. Her uncle's words were challenging, and Esther had to surrender to the fact that her purpose could be down to this very moment. 'If I must die, I must die,' she says when she agrees to go into the king. My dilemma was nowhere near as dramatic or life-threatening as Esther's, but the sense that what was happening might be to benefit someone else really pulled me out of my selfishness. The person who did eventually move in is an amazing girl I now call a friend. She told me the flat was an answer to prayer. Esther's prayerful mission was not for her own benefit. Again, and again, when faced with a situation that I can only see from my perspective, God lifts my head to look afresh at any given scenario from his vantage point. What I saw as a problem, God saw as an opportunity, bringing me into that given situation for 'such a time as this' to bless someone else, blessing me with a brand new friend in the process.

LESSON 26

Misery loves company

When three of Job's friends heard of the tragedy he had suffered, they got together and travelled from their homes to comfort and console him.

—Job 2.11a (NLT)

I first came across the word 'schadenfreude' used in a play in London's West End. It means 'pleasure derived by someone from another person's misfortune.' It was ironic that the friend who took me along to see this play fit this very description rather well. Have you ever tried to tell a friend a story about something you had experienced and listened to them practically jump in with a story of their own? It's usually a comparative tale, intended to show that they know exactly what you mean. If it's a less well-meaning friend, it could also be intended to show how much worse their own experience was, completely overshadowing yours. I'm guilty of this, and I used to have to remind myself not to jump in when I felt like I could completely identify with someone else's experience. Perhaps because of this, I'm perpetually fascinated with the story of Job in the Bible. Having been a 'favourite' of God, he then goes through a horrendous period during which he loses everything, and all he has to support him through that time is a group of friends who, we learn, 'travelled from their homes to comfort and console him'. They sound like good friends who 'sat on the ground with him for seven days and nights' (Job 2.13), but as we see in ensuing verses, their support turns to rebuke as they take turns to tell him why he finds himself in such a desolate position. A few years ago, when I was flat hunting in

London, I found a beautiful apartment sharing with two other similarly aged professionals, but a short conversation told me it wasn't going to work. Both girls were newly single with acrimonious splits behind them, and when they discovered that I was still in the middle of an unwanted divorce, they were thrilled to begin badmouthing their exes, inviting me to join in. At that point, I didn't need any excuse to badmouth my ex, but I also realized that what I really didn't need was to dwell in a pity party. Sometimes we do need to hear each other's traumatic stories or shitty situations, but we need to actually listen to them and try and give them the attention they deserve. When we respond with a situation in kind or try to explain it, all we do is add fuel to the fire. I'm still learning this, and while I love a good party, if pity is the theme, I'm pretty sure God doesn't want me on the guestlist.

LESSON 27

Give them flowers
and give them love

So encourage each other and build each other up, just as you
are already doing.

—1 Thessalonians 5.11 (NLT)

One of my friends is going through a pretty hard time with her ex at
the moment. I've watched her go from unprecedented joy when they
first got together to abject misery when he broke it off. All the conversations we've had involve her wondering what she did wrong – how
she could have done things differently, better. Obviously, I think he's
in the wrong; Nay is beautiful, highly intelligent, thoughtful and
kind. I hate seeing someone I love so sad about someone else not
loving them, and because it's easy to think we see a situation clearly
when we're not in it, my unhelpful advice was to just *move on*. Needless to say, that didn't go down well. Paul's letter to the believers in
Thessalonica is full of encouragement for a people who had become
discouraged. They were living in an area of strong persecution, and
Paul's letters were to comfort them and remind them of God's ulti-
mate victory. None of what Paul was saying was new; he was simply
reaffirming their beliefs so that they would 'encourage each other
and build each other up, just as you are doing'. His letter is kind and
gentle, repeating the use of the phrase 'dear brothers and sisters'; he
doesn't tell the Thessalonians to just 'get over it'. Reading this was
just another reminder of how loving God is and how kind and gentle
his Holy Spirit. After several nights out with Nay, double the amount
of gin and triple my frustration at not 'fixing' her, I realized that all

I could really do is be with her through all the crap and not worry about whether or not she seemed to be getting better. Some days we didn't speak at all, while other days would find her pouring out her heart to me. I responded patiently, making sure I let her grieve, but also reminding her that she would be okay, more than okay. A large, brightly coloured bouquet currently sits on Nay's desk at work, filling the office with its scent. This was my offering, an apology for my lack of understanding and a gift to remind her that she is worthy of them, worthy of flowers and gifts and love. And sometimes that's all we can do for our friends when they're suffering, taking Paul's example and leading with love.

LESSON 28

Honesty friends

In the end, people appreciate honest criticism far more than flattery.

—Proverbs 28.23 (NLT)

I was shopping recently when I received three selfies from my friend, in a dressing room of her own, asking 'What do you think?' I laughed when I got them and knew exactly why she was sending them to me. We all have friends who know how to make us feel really good about things we want to buy, say or do. We know that they will affirm us or our action, so subconsciously, when we present our dilemma to them, we already have an idea of their response. Once when I was deliberating over an expensive pair of boots, it seemed like all the customers around me were encouraging me to buy them. My cousin, who is a personal shopper, said it's because these fellow customers want to feel good about their own purchases and it helps if they feel like someone else is making a similar sacrifice. As a prolific shopper, I have witnessed my share of dishonesty, especially in the changing rooms when sales assistants are just trying to make their commission. But this passage in Proverbs is right; people do appreciate honest criticism far more than flattery. And this extends to far more than just shopping. I always like to be right (who doesn't?) so I'm not great at receiving criticism, but honest criticism is so valuable because it leads to positive change. There is a certain sensitivity you need when telling someone that something isn't going to do them any good. But in the long run, flattery has as much depth as the word might suggest. Whether dismissed as a little white lie or motivated by our own selfish (and often subconscious) gain, flattery isn't high on God's list of qualities to cultivate in our friendships – honesty is, however, so I'm actively trying to wait and reflect before I flatter my friends in all the wrong places.

LESSON 29

Friends who make you feel good

How I weep for you, my brother Jonathan!
Oh, how much I loved you!
And your love for me was deep,
deeper than the love of women!

—2 Samuel 1.26 (NLT)

I have a friend I've known all my life. She lives in another city, but when we see each other, we always eat too much and laugh so much more. The last time I stayed over at hers, we stayed up talking until 5 a.m. in the morning – about everything and nothing. I have another friend who makes me feel cool just by being in her company. I totally dress up for her, and every time we meet, she takes me to some little-known hotspot in London. I learn so much and feel encouraged to be so much more creative just by being around her. Our friends might make good travel buddies, help us sound out ideas, pray for and with us and check in on us if they sense we're feeling low. It's a blessing to be surrounded by such love and kindness, and this blessing of friendship is something that even King David recognized. King David is a well-known biblical figure who had an especially close friendship with King Saul's son Jonathan. They were friends as boys and young men, and David was distraught when Jonathan was killed in battle. His words here in 2 Samuel are a lament composed as part of a funeral song. David was surrounded by strong men appointed as his elite group of fighters (The "thirty"; see 2 Samuel 23.13b) and had many wives and concubines, but we only ever read about this special friendship with Jonathan and how much they meant to each other. A flatmate once told me about one of her good friends and how she always felt judged by her. Even getting ready to meet her made her feel anxious. I know I can be a bit judgemental sometimes, so I tried to consider how friends might feel when they meet up with me. I know I'd be pretty distraught if I thought someone was anxious about spending time together. David and Jonathan seemed to have a friendship without any of those issues. While they may not have agreed on everything – what friends do? – they clearly put their love for each other above all else, and this is the kind of friendship I reach for. The older I get, the more I realize how important it is to cultivate the kinds of friendships we want. Friendships like that of David and Jonathan come when both parties are giving, tolerant and kind. And as we work on being that kind of friend, I believe God will bring people into our lives who reflect that.

LESSON 30

How to let go gracefully

There are 'friends' who destroy each other, but a real friend sticks closer than a brother.

—Proverbs 18.24 (NLT)

Even if you're not looking for it, there are plenty of reminders that best friends should be forever. Pinterest spews out quotes for BFFs; split heart chains for 'Best Friends' or 'Best B*tches' are now sold for teenagers and adults alike, and Facebook throws up our friendship history with unrequested frequency. I grew up reading books echoing this penchant for forever friends so when I made my own, I was delighted. I was quite bossy with my teenage bestie, perhaps making up for feelings of inadequacy at home; I insisted we dress the same, and at one point we even had matching cars. Growing up with the kind of bosom buddies depicted in my Judy Blume books, I didn't expect any of my close friendships to end, but it is inherent in this scripture that some friendships do, and some friendships should. Where there are 'friends who destroy each other', there are 'real' friends who stick 'closer than a brother'. Though not all of us have close relationships with our siblings, we probably all share the sense that shared life and being part of the same family – even as brothers and sisters in Christ – offer a greater opportunity for closeness than some transient friendships. But the scripture also warns of the influence close relationships have to 'destroy' one another. I was unimpressed when my mum suggested that I was a 'bad influence' on my own car-twinning bestie. However, as we slowly drifted apart, I realized how controlling I had been in our relationship and how her naturally quiet disposition meant she would rarely make her own decisions about what was best for her. I wasn't out to 'destroy' her, but ultimately our friendship was not one built to last. I don't read the two statements in this passage as opposites; I don't think that you're either a bad influence or a best friend for life. But I do think that we come across both types on our life journey and that it's important to recognize both so that we can protect our relationships accordingly. The Bible's talk of seasons and King Solomon's account in Ecclesiastes 3 also remind us that it's important to recognize that things change. Just like some romantic relationships, some friends are only in our lives for a season. So, if you find yourself in this position, my advice would be twofold: First of all, remember the cheesy but true saying 'Don't cry because it's over, laugh because it happened.' And second, take the opportunity to buy some new friendship jewellery.

Section Four

Lessons from family

I was born into a pretty standard nuclear family. My sister came first, and I have a younger brother too. But shortly before he was born, our parents split up and consequently divorced. This was a huge upheaval to us all as our house was sold, and our parents went their separate ways. As is still pretty common, we went to live with Mum, seeing Dad during the school holidays. A sensitive child, I felt everything keenly, and this new set-up changed how I viewed myself and the world around me.

My stability was shaken, and I lost, if I ever had it, that sense of unconditional love. I'm eternally grateful to my mum for taking us to church, which is where I really started to feel that strong sense of family. The message I felt up until then was that family was what you had unless you decided you didn't like the people in it. I love the scripture in Matthew 12.50 where Jesus says, 'For whoever does the will of my Father in heaven is my brother and sister and mother' (NLT). Contrary to what I had learned growing up, in the church, family is family regardless of how you feel about the people in it.

Ultimately, our experience of family provides a powerful backdrop for how we approach things in adulthood, especially faith, as God is painted as both father and mother in the Bible. These lessons are an exploration into what family might mean to all of us – the family we are given and the family we choose – and what God has to say about each of these.

LESSON 31

Be your brother's (and sister's) keeper

Afterward the LORD asked Cain,
'Where is your brother? Where is Abel?'
'I don't know,' Cain responded.
'Am I my brother's guardian?'

—Genesis 4.9 (NLT)

Yes, Cain; yes, you are. Extrovert or introvert, I truly believe that humans weren't created to be alone. Data released by the Office of National Statistics in 2018 revealed that people of all ages are at risk from diseases brought on by loneliness, with 2.4 million adult British residents suffering from chronic loneliness. Researchers found that loneliness is associated with a 50 per cent increase in mortality from any cause, and as a result, the UK government published a strategy to tackle loneliness in October 2018. We might understand this feeling of isolation in older generations, especially if they are retired, widowed and/or with no close family members. But these days, even those of us with full-time jobs, flat sharing in cosmopolitan cities, can feel lonely and isolated. The first Christmas I spent alone after my divorce was horrible. I was disconnected from my in-laws who were big Christmas people and was still struggling to reconnect to my own family, having become estranged when I got married. I remember people asking what I was doing, and when I replied that I was spending it alone, the responses were usually something along the lines of 'Oh lucky you' and 'I wish I didn't have to spend it with my awful in-laws!' Not one person asked if it was my choice, and it wasn't. This scripture gives witness to the first murder in the Bible. Cain has murdered his brother out of jealousy, but what caught me reading this is his reply to God. When asked where his brother is, Cain's response is dismissive, nonchalant: 'Am I my brother's guardian?' He is, in effect, absolving himself of all responsibility for Abel's whereabouts. We know from Hebrews 13.1, which reads 'Keep on loving each other as brothers and sisters', that the bond between siblings should be a strong one – which is what makes Cain's reaction so wrong. At Christmas and other significant milestones through the year, many of us will prioritize family, but I hope that we would also look outside of our immediate family members and reach out to our other 'brothers and sisters', especially those who might have nowhere else to go.

LESSON 32

The power of praise

> I will praise the LORD at all times. I will constantly speak his
> praises.
> I will boast only in the LORD; let all who are helpless take heart.
> Come, let us tell of the LORD's greatness; let us exalt his name
> together.
>
> —Psalm 34.1–3 (NLT)

One thing my family gave me was a passion for praise. I'm not sure
if this was the same for you and yours, but growing up in a musical family, we often sang and worshipped God together – coerced
or otherwise. Between us, we played the piano, French horn, violin,
drums, guitar and recorder. My mum was of the opinion that televi-
sion was the 'enemy of progress', refusing to have one in the house,
and so music was a key form of entertainment for me as a child.
During my teens, we went through a particularly difficult period as
a family, and my mum insisted that we get up early to praise God
for an hour before we got ready for our day. I resented this at first
and would have much preferred to spend this extra hour in bed,
but Mum's children tended to do as they were told. Though I was
frustrated by what I saw as interruption to my sleep, I recognized
something beautiful and sacrificial in starting our days that way and
could sense an uplifting in my spirit and closeness to God. In 1 Samuel 16.14–23, we read the story of how David provided musical ther-
apy for King Saul. Displeased with the actions of King Saul, we read
that 'the Lord sent a tormenting spirit that filled him with depression and fear,' and some of his servants suggested they find a good

musician to play the harp: 'He will play soothing music, and you will soon be well again.' David, 'a fine-looking young man', is brought to King Saul, and we read 'And whenever the tormenting spirit from God troubled Saul, David would play the harp. Then Saul would feel better and the tormenting spirit would go away.' In Psalms such as the one above, David, now king, is known to praise God in both victory and helplessness: 'I will praise the Lord at all times. I will constantly speak his praises.' He knows that praising God is how we can honour him, but he also recognizes that we too benefit because musical praise brings us joy and into closer relationship with him.

LESSON 33

Set your own tone

Then you will experience God's peace, which exceeds anything we can understand. His peace will guard your hearts and minds as you live in Christ Jesus.

—Philippians 4.7 (NLT)

When my mother was my age, she already had three children and was divorced from our father. As a single parent, she was a strong maternal figure who often dominated the atmosphere at home. On the rare occasions she was sick, the entire house was shrouded in a cloak of darkness, as the curtains stayed down and the table lay bare. When she was happy, joy radiated through all of us – the windows were flung open to embrace the outside, and up-tempo music reverberated through every room. And when she was angry, a startled, pin-drop silence was all there was. As a child, you often think that the world revolves around you, so when a parent or carer behaves in a certain way, we automatically think we are the cause. I never dared to ask my mum what was wrong on those sad and bad days, but I'm pretty sure I was not (always) the reason. And yet, as a sensitive child, her moods affected me hugely. I took this into adulthood and would always try to assess the tone of a room before I entered it so that I could respond appropriately. I can spot an alpha figure instantly, and a sharp response from a colleague at work would send me scuttling meekly away, feeling fearful and unsettled. Have you ever felt like that – as though you aren't quite sure whether you are where you should be, or how to cope in certain situations? For me, this just meant that I was always on high alert, ready to pre-empt any mood changes, and those who do the same will know how exhausting this is. I really feared conflict and longed for the peace described in this scripture. I became a Christian as a teenager, but it wasn't until my early twenties that I learned that it is possible to have this peace 'which exceeds anything we can understand', even when everything around us seems volatile and unstable. Daily devotionals can help with this, and while some days we might regress to old childhood behaviour, it's important not to beat ourselves up about it – old habits can take a while to shake off. The key is to stop allowing others to determine the tone of our environment. God should be the only one to do that, and his peace is the atmosphere we should seek to surround us.

LESSON 34

The power in our words

Out of the same mouth come praise and cursing. My brothers and sisters, this should not be.

—James 3.10 (NIV)

It is becoming widely acknowledged that the words we speak can actually change the course of our lives. This starts from when we are very young – the words spoken over us in childhood to the words of teachers, colleagues, friends and partners as we get older. Do you remember that playground rhyme: 'Sticks and stones may break my bones, but words will never hurt me'? I'm presuming it was created to empower children affected by bullying, but this is not a statement I can agree with because while bones generally heal and scars fade, words can stay with you forever. Recently, I made a list of the words people have spoken 'over me', both as a child and adult, and I realized that while I could usually brush off the ones I heard as an adult, the negative ones in my childhood from close family members seemed to have a greater hold on me. One morning when praying, I felt God speak to me about how I used my words both to myself and to others. I was in the middle of writing this book, and a friend had told me she felt I would be a teacher – not in a classroom, but for God's word – and as James says in verse 1 of this chapter, 'we who teach will be judged more strictly.' Numbers 6.22–27 is an example of how God uses his words, and it is to bless, not to curse: 'The Lord said to Moses, "Tell Aaron and his sons, 'This is how you are to bless the Israelites. Say to them: "The Lord bless you and keep you; the Lord make his face shine on you and be gracious to you; the Lord turn his face toward you and give you peace."""" Being given the opportunity to share God's word is always an honour, but knowing how power-fully words follow us into adulthood, that honour also comes with great responsibility, and for me that responsibility from God is to use my words to bless and not curse.

LESSON 35

We should all be 'mums'

While Jesus was still talking to the crowd, his mother and brothers stood outside, wanting to speak to him. Someone told him, 'Your mother and brothers are standing outside, wanting to speak to you.' He replied to him, 'Who is my mother, and who are my brothers?' Pointing to his disciples, he said, 'Here are my mother and my brothers. For whoever does the will of my Father in heaven is my brother and sister and mother.'

—Matthew 12.46–50 (NIV)

I once had the honour of looking after two little girls from time to time while their mum, a single parent with two other children, had some time to herself. It made me laugh just to be around these wonderful little beings, so inquisitive and prone to ridiculous outbursts if they didn't get their own way – traits I still employ from time to time. I made sure they were clothed and fed, helped potty train the eldest and endured endless repetition in games and activities. It was a labour of love. On one occasion, when they were with their mum, I opened the door to the room they were in and the youngest, around 13 months at the time, immediately climbed down off her mum's lap and toddled over to me. When I opened my arms to pick her up, she fell into them and rested her head on my shoulders. Even though she wasn't my child, I believe she knew that I had grown to love her, and her overworked mum was instantly reassured that she was leaving her child in good hands. When we talk about 'family', we usually mean those of us to whom we are related by blood. Sometimes in church, we refer to fellow Christians as our sisters and brothers, and some have 'spiritual mothers/fathers' who are older members of the church who might be our mentors. This means we are part of a church family as Jesus alludes to in this scripture, 'Here are my mother and my brothers. For whoever does the will of my Father in heaven is my brother and sister and mother.' It is the responsibility and honour of a family to help and support one another, and we have a great opportunity to do that with each other's children. One of my friends who doesn't want children of her own has about ten godchildren on which she is able to dote time and attention in a way she wouldn't be able if she had ten children of her own. I'm not suggesting we take the place of actual parents or carers – if they have them – but whether in a crèche, or as an aunt or godparent, children benefit when they interact with us all. So next time you see a parent struggling with a screaming child in the supermarket or an over-active child at church who won't stay still, try and resist the urge to judge and maybe ask if you can help. There's an African proverb, 'it takes a village to raise a child,' and God has called us to support each other as if we were one family because to him, we are.

LESSON 36

Humility precedes honour

When Bathsheba went to King Solomon to speak to him for
Adonijah, the king stood up to meet her, bowed down to her
and sat down on his throne. He had a throne brought for the
king's mother, and she sat down at his right hand.

—1 Kings 2.19

My father is from the Yoruba tribe in Nigeria, and one of the cultural
practices is to kneel or bow before someone older or of greater
importance. We don't practice it that strongly in my family, and it's
a concept which might seem more than a little outdated, but reading this passage in 1 Kings made me see things differently. In the
Bible, a king or queen would be used to having other people bow
down before them, and earlier in this chapter we see how Bathsheba,
Solomon's mother, bows to King David, her husband (1 King 1.15
and 1.31) in keeping with the customs of the time. King Solomon
took the throne after his father, and we read in this scripture: 'When
Bathsheba went to King Solomon to speak to him for Adonijah, the
king stood up to meet her, bowed down to her and sat down on his
throne. He had a throne brought for the king's mother, and she sat
down at his right hand.' In the Bible, for someone to be seated at the
right hand, is a sign of power. King Solomon is showing deference to
his mother and following the commandment to 'honour your father
and mother' (Matt. 19.19 NLT). As I read this scripture in 1 Kings, I
remembered Bathsheba's back story and how King David basically
had her husband killed so that he could have her for himself. Because
of David's sin, God sent a deadly virus to the child Bathsheba was

carrying and he died. As king, her living child was able to honour her in front of everyone. I don't kneel or bow before my parents and if I did, we would all think it was pretty weird. But recently I was on a bus and recognized an elderly Nigerian woman with the tribal scars that characterize my father's people. She was sitting upright and looked so regal, even among the noise and dirt of London's public transport systems. As I watched her, I suddenly had the urge to bow before her and show her the respect she deserved. As the bus came to my stop, I paused before I got off, turned to the woman, looked into her eyes to catch her attention and then dipped my head and body slowly to bow before her. I could almost feel the silence as people stared in surprise, but as I stood up, she smiled, nodded at me and said, 'God bless you.' It was a small interaction, but it gave me some insight into where King Solomon was coming from. It felt good to honour her and the blessing that came after was an added bonus. Whether it is your parents, carers or older members of your church or community, we should all take time out of our day to honour someone, the way God intended.

LESSON 37

Intentional adulthood

Let your roots grow down into him, and let your lives be built on him. Then your faith will grow strong in the truth you were taught, and you will overflow with thankfulness.

—Colossians 2.7 (NLT)

A few years ago, my childhood friend bumped into my mum while out shopping. Apparently the conversation went something like this.

FRIEND: 'Hi Auntie, how are you?' (African culture dictates that anyone older than you, relative or not, is referred to as 'Auntie' or 'Uncle')

MUM: 'Hi, are you still single? Why are none of you married yet?' I have long since learned – as so many of us have – that much of the older generation expects me to have been married for a while now. I ran with this idea growing up and decided that by the time I reached my mid-twenties, I would be married with children. For me, it wasn't so much a life choice as a life slide. I figured as soon as I was 'ready' (whatever that meant), I would get to the top of the metaphorical slide and with one push, off I would go, gravity pulling me easily to the land of married people with babies. I never considered how that would affect my life, purpose, personal goals – or even my faith. There are many people who grow up wanting to be a full-time mum and/or housewife; there's intention in that goal and that's great. I've also met a few parents who say they wish they had been more intentional about getting married and having children, rather than letting it be what is considered a 'natural' next step. Without the joys and responsibilities of long-term commitments attributed to partners and children, many can feel left without the same common markers with which to consider the true trajectory of their lives. In this scripture, Paul is writing a letter to some believers while he was in prison. He urges them 'let your roots grow down into him', something I failed to do in my assumption that mine would simply follow the tracks laid down for me by parents, society and even the Church. As women today, many of us have the benefits our ancestors didn't; we can make our own money, our own decisions. And there is so much beauty in building our lives on Jesus – finding out what he has to say about us and discovering our gifts and talents. Being intentional in this way just means that our faith has a chance to develop, even if on the outside nothing seems to be changing and the milestones we associate with 'family' don't appear forthcoming. I admit I find it annoying when churches expect single people to be free to get involved in church activities. But actually, this is a good way to get involved with another family – our church family. And we can learn many lessons there for when/if we have children of our own. Either way, we can use this time to carve out who and why we are – revelling in the joy of now. And then one day when you look back, you'll undoubtedly find yourself doing that annoying auntie thing of declaring to yourself, 'My, how you've grown!'

LESSON 38
Go for it

They came back to Moses and Aaron and the whole Israelite community at Kadesh in the Desert of Paran. There they reported to them and to the whole assembly and showed them the fruit of the land. They gave Moses this account: 'We went into the land to which you sent us, and it does flow with milk and honey! Here is its fruit. But the people who live there are powerful and the cities are fortified and very large. We even saw descendants of Anak there. The Amalekites live in the Negev; the Hittites, Jebusites and Amorites live in the hill country; and the Canaanites live near the sea and along the Jordan.' Then Caleb silenced the people before Moses and said, 'We should go up and take possession of the land, for we can certainly do it.' But the men who had gone up with him said, 'We can't attack those people; they are stronger than we are.' And they spread among the Israelites a bad report about the land they had explored. They said, 'The land we explored devours those living in it. All the people we saw there are of great size. We saw the Nephilim there (the descendants of Anak come from the Nephilim). We seemed like grasshoppers in our own eyes, and we looked the same to them.'

—Numbers 13.26–33 (NIV)

I recently came across an old email from my mum. It was a reply to one from me where I told her I was nervous about an upcoming interview. I was fresh out of university, and this would be my first full-time role. Mum's reply was simply, 'Remember the ten spies and the "giants"... go for it, no matter how it looks!' That email was sent years ago, and at her advice, I did go for that job, and I got it. Verses 1–2 give us the back story to this scripture in Numbers: 'The Lord said to Moses, "Send some men to explore the land of Canaan, which I am giving to the Israelites. From each ancestral tribe send one of its leaders."' After 40 days spent checking out the territory, most of the spies returned excited about the beauty and potential of the land but terrified of its current inhabitants, who were giants. Caleb tries to rescue the situation by reminding them of the fact that God had actually promised them this land back when they were still slaves in Egypt (Exod. 3.8) but his appeal, 'We should go up and take possession of the land, for we can certainly do it,' is silenced by his fellow explorers who begin to spread the fear even more by telling people how inferior they were to the people living in the land. Someone once pointed out to me that the men who returned with this negative feedback were so focused on how small they seemed compared with the giants, they neglected to consider the powerful, miracle-working God who had told them the land was theirs for the taking. They saw the obstacle, but not the weapon (God) they had with which to fight. I'm so grateful to my mum for her knowledge of God's word and her example of applying it to our own lives as fits the promise from God in Psalm 32.8, 'I will instruct you and teach you in the way you should go; I will counsel you with my loving eye on you.' Are there older and wiser people speaking into your life today, reminding you of all the promises that are ours to hold on to?

LESSON 39

What's in a name?

No longer will you be called Abram;* your name will be Abraham,** for I have made you a father of many nations.

—Genesis 17.5 (NIV)

*Abram means 'high father'
**Abraham sounds like a Hebrew term that means 'father of many nations'

Nigerians believe that when you call people by their name, you are speaking into their lives, so the meaning is deemed particularly important. Some names are literal, and so you'll find many people of West African origin named Blessing or Favour. It is also common to name children around the circumstances of their birth or to connect them to their heritage. My full Nigerian name is Omotola which translates as 'to have a child is to have wealth'. I never met my maternal grandma Stella, but I'm told she also gave me the English name Patricia. I've never liked it, but recently I decided to check out the meaning behind the name she picked for me. The Bible gives eight verses to God renaming Abraham, and he renamed him as a sign of the covenant he was making, saying 'This is my covenant with you: I will make you the father of a multitude of many nations! What's more, I am changing your name. It will no longer be Abram. Instead you will be called Abraham for you will be the father of many nations.' This powerful covenant came with it a change of identity even though Abraham himself would not get to see the multitudes that would be his descendants. Every time someone called

Abraham by his name, they would be reminding him of the promise of God over his life. Patricia comes from the word 'patrician' meaning 'noble', a word defined as 'belonging by rank, title or birth to the aristocracy'. Grandma Stella never met me, never knew what kind of person I would become, but she knew that I was being raised in a country which historically looked down on those with our skin colour. She had lived here while at finishing school, and maybe she received that treatment herself despite a background of high importance back home. Grandma sent my mum a letter with this name, and while she didn't articulate it, Mum felt that she had recently become a believer, so the name might also represent her wish to remind me that I was a child of God and therefore daughter of a king. It might not be that your parents chose your name to bestow any particular meaning, but I can guarantee there are people in your family – whether related by blood or faith – who want to speak words of encouragement or instil prayers and hopes into your life. Like I did with my Grandma Stella, is it time for you to probe into your past and find out?

LESSON 40

Home sweet home

My people will live in peaceful dwelling-places,
   in secure homes,
   in undisturbed places of rest.

—Isaiah 32.18 (NIV)

Some of you may have moved around a lot in childhood, or maybe you never felt as though you really had a home. For me personally, home is really important. I'm currently living in what is my tenth home, and friends were surprised when I started completely redecorating immediately after I moved in. I'm sure an expert would put this down to my parents' divorce and feeling a distinct lack of stability; maybe I create adult versions of the sheet-covered hideaways we built as children? Some of us may want to provide the type of family home we longed for as children. I just think that home for me is intrinsically linked to my desire to belong. This 32nd chapter in Isaiah is about Israel's deliverance, and the book itself rests on the central theme of salvation, with God redeeming his people from Egypt and captivity. The words of this particular verse, 'My people will live in peaceful dwelling places, in secure homes, in undisturbed places of rest,' are a reminder of what we ultimately hope for in salvation: a place of rest with God. Many Christians talk about those who have died as having 'gone home', home to be with God where there is no more sickness or pain (Rev. 7.15–17, 21.4). In John 14.2, Jesus continues this concept of heaven as home as he tells his disciples, 'My Father's house has many rooms; if that were not so, would I have told you that I am going there to prepare a place for you?' If the number of home- and property-related programmes is anything to go by, we are all a bit obsessed with our homes right now, and I wonder if it's partly because everything outside of it feels so unsteady. Technology gives us open access to all that is going on in the world – the sickness, the battles, the crime, the injustice. Perhaps our interest in creating a home for ourselves is because we're all just tired and want a safe space where everything feels okay. But ultimately, what we have here on earth isn't really home. Ezekiel 28.25 reads, 'This is what the Sovereign Lord says: When I gather the people of Israel from the nations where they have been scattered, I will be proved holy through them in the sight of the nations. Then they will live in their own land, which I gave to my servant Jacob.' Like the Israelites who spent so many years as wanderers, God calls us into his family, and the promised land is the home we long for.

Section Five

Lessons from marriage

I was married and divorced by the time I was 30, and I honestly felt like God had left me out to dry. I had experienced the highs of becoming and being part of a married couple and the lows of feeling as if I had lost my best friend. Writing in retrospect, it might seem as though the lows of this period are more visible. But I think it's important to say that I really did love my ex-husband, and that's why these lessons have played such an integral part of the healing process for me. God really does work everything for good, even if we don't see it yet.

You'll understand by now that I'm a bit of a speed head, racing through everything in order to get to what I saw as the 'best part'. The biggest lesson from this area of my life was about timing and learning that whether we are waiting for a partner, a husband, a job or a baby, we pay a high cost for impatience. God gives us a good example of this in the story of Isaac and Ishmael in the Bible. Ishmael was the child that Abraham and Sarah brought about in their own strength. Even though God's promise of Isaac did come later, the lines between the two heirs had already been drawn. Their haste cost their descendants the peace of a God-given single heir and family line. In my case, speeding ahead may have cost me my marriage. God's timing is not our timing, and even when he shares something about our future, we need to use all of our God-enabled willpower not to try and force it to happen in our own strength.

LESSON 41

'We kind of didn't get on'

Place me like a seal over your heart,
  like a seal on your arm.
For love is as strong as death,
  its jealousy as enduring as the grave.

—Song of Songs 8.6 (NLT)

'We kind of didn't get on' were the words used as the heading for Fish's[1] and my wedding announcement in *The Times*. We had met as colleagues and did not look like a match made in heaven. His work persona displayed as arrogant, and because I left on time each day, he saw me as work-shy. Having previously been in love with someone who was a fellow Christian and Nigerian and having had the relationship not work out, it didn't even cross my mind that an English, non-believing partner could be a good match. I remained friends with my team after leaving the company, but Fish and I had still never really spoken so I was surprised when, a few months after I left, he came out of a group chat to send me a private message telling me he and his girlfriend had broken up. The move from uninterested to relationship was a journey that seemed to creep up on me, if not for him. He told me later that he had been desperate for me to know he was single and that he knew we were going to be together. Fish chose this scripture in Song of Songs for our wedding ceremony. This is a common wedding reading, but in choosing this passage, I felt

---

1   I've called my ex-husband 'Fish' in this book as it was my nickname for him in our early time together as a couple.

the strength with which he was committing himself to me, having also committed himself to God a few months into our relationship. Love here is described as a 'seal' and unquenchable, its 'jealousy unyielding as the grave'. In other parts of the Bible we read that God is love (1 John 4.7) and that God is a jealous God (Exod. 20.5b). This passage echoes that sense of the power of God's love for us. God's 'jealousy' is not like the world's jealousy; it is not mean or harmful but determined as he reaches out to every one of us with a deep love that we can wear like a seal as we share it with others. Not too long ago, I felt God showing me a picture which demonstrated that no matter how far removed two people might be from each other, no matter how different their paths, if God wills it, he can reach out and draw them together with his love. And I believe this is what happened with Fish and me; we may have started off as enemies, but I really do believe God brought us together to be more than just friends.

LESSON 42
His perfect timing

Yet God has made everything beautiful for its own time. He has planted eternity in the human heart, but even so, people cannot see the whole scope of God's work from beginning to end.

—Ecclesiastes 3.11 (NLT)

I could tell my mum liked Fish, and his mum liked me. We spent a lot of time with his family but not so much with mine because, as much as Mum liked Fish as an individual, she wasn't keen on us actually being together. The relationship between mother-in-law and son-in-law can be tricky to navigate, although she didn't articulate her objection much while we were just dating. But when he proposed, she told me she couldn't be happy for me. Naturally, this caused a rift in our mother-daughter relationship, which was already fraught from recent teenage-parent struggles. The frustrating thing for me was Mum not being able to explain what she saw as the problem. Fish sensibly suggested we hold off on actually getting married until my mum was on board, but I was angry that she should dictate *my* marriage, *my* happiness. Traditionally, Nigerian parents expect their children to obey them all the way into adulthood, so there was an element of my mum not feeling she needed to explain herself to me. But I was headstrong, in love and I honestly sensed that God was in our relationship, so for the first time in my life, I said no to her. Impatience has always been part of my character (even though we were only engaged for 18 months, I walked down the aisle to Etta James's *At Last*), and I'm a planner, so once I have an idea in mind, I like to get on with it. This kind of go-getter attitude is often exalted as a strength; there's no time like the present, right? But what if there was a better time than right now and we just can't see it yet? This scripture written by King Solomon, recorded as the wisest man in the Bible, reminds me that there is so much going on 'behind the scenes' of what we perceive. Our engagement didn't seem rushed to us, but I see now that the foundations for our marriage had not yet been cemented. I have never truly felt that our marriage was a mistake but have wondered whether we were ready for each other as husband and wife. We still had so much to learn. During the difficult period that was our engagement, my late pastor's wife, who was a rock throughout it all, told me that God was using our marriage as an example. 'An example of what?' I wondered at the time. Now, the words in this passage made me realize that it was an example that even if you have all the love in the world and all seems right, timing is everything. I have no idea if Mum would have changed her mind in the end or if we would have stayed together if the timing were different, but I do know that our marriage is an example of what happens when you don't let God make everything beautiful in its time.

LESSON 43

Soulmates

The man said,
'This is now bone of my bones
    and flesh of my flesh;
she shall be called "woman,"
    for she was taken out of man.'
For this reason a man will leave his father and mother and be
united to his wife, and they will become one flesh.

—Genesis 2.23–24 (NIV)

I'm not sure if I ever really believed in soulmates, but if they do exist, then I found one in Fish. He used to say we were like two of the same person. The night we first started speaking properly, when I went back to my old workplace for a leaving do, is a distant memory now. But I do remember someone looking between the two of us and saying, 'you two are going to end up together.' Of course, everyone laughed it off because of our history – we had never seen eye to eye. But that observant colleague was right, and I loved being Fish's wife. I loved hearing him run up the stairs to our apartment followed by his key turning in the door, knowing I would soon be held tightly in his arms. We were a tactile couple, and I recall annoying other customers by refusing to let go of each other's hands while we pushed our shopping trolley down the aisle in Tesco. It sounds improbable now, but I couldn't quite work the Sky remote when I first moved in, so he wrote down instructions on post-it notes. This started off a practice of leaving notes for each other. When Fish left before me in the mornings, he would leave a note wishing me a good day and reminding me that he loved me. If I was coming home late, I would leave a note for him to read when he got home from work, telling him to enjoy watching all the things I hated: sports and horror films. And most importantly, reminding him that I loved him. He loved seeing me happy, and I wanted to give him everything I had so that he could be happy too. This scripture in Genesis shows that Adam and his wife really were made for each other: 'This is now bone of my bones and flesh of my flesh.' Adam knew that the other creatures he was presented with simply wouldn't do. Eve was literally a part of him, and Adam sensed that – something Fish and I felt in our most tender moments as husband and wife. I think we've misinterpreted this, in our modern age. We say things like 'our better/other half' to describe the person we are in love with. I don't agree with this terminology; I believe God has created us as whole beings. But I do know that my life was enhanced with Fish in it. And unlike the 'once in a lifetime' soulmates glorified by so many of our romantic comedies, I believe God is powerful enough to bind my whole self together with another's whole self if that is God's perfect will for us.

LESSON 44

Free will

The servant asked him, 'What if the woman is unwilling to come back with me to this land? Shall I then take your son back to the country you came from?'

'Make sure that you do not take my son back there,' Abraham said. 'The LORD, the God of heaven, who brought me out of my father's household and my native land and who spoke to me and promised me on oath, saying, "To your offspring I will give this land" – he will send his angel before you so that you can get a wife for my son from there. If the woman is unwilling to come back with you, then you will be released from this oath of mine. Only do not take my son back there.'

—Genesis 24.5–8 (NIV)

On the evening of our wedding day, I lay in bed with my new husband beside me and thought I had never felt so happy. As I went over the intimate details of the day – even the things that had gone wrong – I couldn't help but feel that everything was as it should be. A dear friend had sent me a text to say she felt God was pleased with our marriage, and I believed it. I was in love with a man who loved me back, and I felt like the luckiest girl in the world. I've explained how I fell in love with words at a young age; to me, a person's word was their bond, so I found it difficult to comprehend times when people reneged on commitments. This chapter continues the story of Abraham and opens with him asking a long-serving servant to go to his hometown and bring back a wife for Isaac. The servant seems understandably nervous about having to separate a woman from her family in order to marry into one she has never met. He asks Abraham what he should do if the woman is unwilling. What if she says no? It was and still is a strange concept for me: the idea that God could ordain something, only for the person or people involved to be unwilling. But Abraham's reply reminds me that both things can be possible: 'he [God] will send his angel before you so that you can get a wife for my son from there. If the woman is unwilling to come back with you, then you will be released from this oath of mine.' I never had any doubts about marrying Fish and was encouraged by the friend who shared what she felt was a stamp of approval from the Holy Spirit. Not long after Annie died, Fish went on a two-week silent retreat. He felt that he really needed the space to tap into what was going on in his head. I waited patiently, anxiously and was relieved when he returned and said confidently that he was surer than ever about us. But less than a month later, he told me he wanted a divorce. I couldn't understand it for a long, long time. How could someone be so sure about something and then completely turn his back on it? It wasn't until I read this passage in Genesis that I felt a glimpse of how things might look from another view. Just like Abraham explained to his servant, if the person involved is unwilling, then he was no longer under oath. God may have breathed life into our marriage, but we both had free will to decide what to do with it. When marriages and relationships end against our will, we can feel completely broken. But in time we will see that what this also means is that we can actively partake in the release from that commitment. And we are also free – free to start over and love again.

LESSON 45

It's not you, it's me

They are like trees planted by a riverbank,
  bearing fruit each season.
Their leaves never wither,
  and they prosper in all they do.

—Psalm 1.3 (NLT)

I'm going to go out on a limb and say I assume I'm not alone in my tendency to romanticize past relationships. I went through a period of doing it obsessively with my ex-husband. It's true that the only people who know what really goes on in a relationship are the people actually in it. I really felt this as the months passed following the divorce settlement, and well-meaning friends queried why we were still in touch. I remember being in a small group meeting with some people from church and trying to explain why I felt Fish and I were just 'meant to be'. I told them how comfortable I felt around him even while we were separated, recounting one early morning where I started singing and worshipping God while in bed with him silent and listening beside me. Even though at that point his position on faith was very different from mine, I hadn't felt any awkwardness in expressing my faith that way, and I took that as a sign of how comfortable he made me. But it was only when I started to recollect similarly freeing experiences in other relationships that I realized the common denominator in each situation was me. *I* was the reason I felt free to be myself no matter whom I was with, and this openness helped that freedom to have a two-way flow. 'They are like trees planted by a riverbank, bearing fruit each season' reminds me of one of my favourite sayings: Bloom where you're planted. The saying echoes this scripture which recognizes that God's people will flourish in all situations. If we don't allow ourselves to recognize this blessing, we can wrongly use these experiences to justify why we should be with someone, using it to explain to doubters why we are a good fit. But the 'fit' comes from walking with God and being given the freedom to 'bear fruit each season'. It might not be for you, but it was a huge revelation to me, realizing that at some point on my journey getting to know God and myself, I had become someone whose leaves 'never wither'. This means that no matter which person I am with, I continue to emanate that same freedom – whether that is singing out loud to God while my partner lies next to me or something else which might seem a bit awkward – because it's just part of who I am; who we all are when we are living in Christ. I hope this gives you hope that as long as you stay connected to God, like a tree close to the life-giving water from the river, your leaves will never wither.

LESSON 46
The D-word

When they reached the place God had told him about, Abraham built an altar there and arranged the wood on it. He bound his son Isaac and laid him on the altar, on top of the wood. Then he reached out his hand and took the knife to slay his son. But the angel of the LORD called out to him from heaven, 'Abraham! Abraham!'

'Here I am,' he replied.

'Do not lay a hand on the boy,' he said. 'Do not do anything to him. Now I know that you fear God, because you have not withheld from me your son, your only son.'

—Genesis 22.9–12 (NIV)

Both Fish and I have divorced parents, and so we were adamant that our marriage wouldn't end the same way. Why would it? We were so sure about each other. But something shifted shortly after we got married as if a light had gone out. We had several big fights, but initially, what felt like a deep love for each other and a strong will to see things through seemed to carry us. But when I stopped going to church and he stopped talking about God – two things which had been strong features of our early relationship – I could feel Fish withdrawing from me, from us. When Fish told me he wanted to meet with his solicitors, I hid our marriage certificate, knowing that he couldn't file for divorce without it. If it sounds desperate, it's because I was, and when he eventually filed for divorce, I fought it with everything I could. I prayed, fasted, believed, argued with Fish and pleaded with God. Our conflict sent me running back to God and back to church. Every Monday evening, I would make the long trip from our marital home to my old church to just pray and worship God with other believers. Not many people knew what was going on at home, but one day the prayer leader read this scripture in Genesis and said he felt God was asking me to lay my marriage on the altar, just like Abraham did. Abraham had no guarantees that God would provide an alternative sacrifice. He was obedient with the thing he held most dear, that held utmost importance for him. His son had been God's promise to him and God had fulfilled that promise, so it seemed odd that he would take that away by the boy's early death. We know from the beginning of the story how it ends, but Abraham had no such assurance. When the divorce seemed to be taking longer than it should have, I felt that might be a sign that it wouldn't happen, so I continued sleeping with Fish even while the divorce papers were going back and forth, in the hope that the closeness would keep us together and he would change his mind. Sexual intimacy really does bond in a way nothing else does. But eventually, Fish sat me down and told me that while he loved me and that all he wanted to do was take me in his arms and make everything okay, he still wanted a divorce. I let go then; I left our marriage there with God, trusting him as Abraham did, right at the altar. This is obviously a very personal decision, but I urge you, if you're fighting for something which seems like a lost cause – just give it to God, and he will work it out for you and give you exactly what you need.

LESSON 47

Be kind to yourself

The LORD says, 'I will rescue those who love me.
   I will protect those who trust in my name.
When they call on me, I will answer;
   I will be with them in trouble.
   I will rescue and honor them.
I will reward them with a long life
   and give them my salvation.'

—Psalm 91.14–16 (NLT)

I spent the year or two after my divorce drunk. I became queen of 'out, out', and my social media was full of the evidence of my antics. I didn't really drink in my teens, so in some ways it felt like a late rite of passage. I hardly slept, lost about a stone and spent all my money on holidays and new clothes. I'm sure people felt I was being irresponsible. Having just come out of a divorce, maybe I should have focused on getting my life together, buying a home for myself and getting ready for whatever was next. But the truth is I just couldn't. All my activity was the momentum I needed to stop myself from facing my harsh reality. Among the Christian naysayers who considered themselves well within their rights to tell me I was living a sinful life, I remember one friend repeating these words to me: 'Be kind to yourself.' Psalm 91 is a psalm of protection that I memorized in adolescence, and it is a constant reminder that God alone is my place of safety. Prior to this, when I had read about God helping or supporting us through difficult situations, as here in verse 15, 'I will be with them in trouble' or the valley of the shadow of death in

Psalm 23.4, I hadn't quite recognized that this includes self-inflicted circumstances. I could not stop the divorce, but not everyone would have taken the destructive path that I set on in its wake. Looking back, I can see I had been protected in those dangerous situations I found myself in. What my friend saw is what God knew, that at the heart of my self-destruction was a deep cry for God and his love. I was hurtling through my own deep valley, and only God knew how to rescue me in a way which meant that I would come out safely through the other side. Perhaps our job as Christians is not to try and be perfect in all ways at all times, but to go running to the only one who knows what to do with our pain. For reasons best known to myself and God, this was how I managed to struggle through and find my way back to him. I encourage you today – if you're running towards alcohol or partying or boys to fill the yearning in your heart meant for God – to turn to him with all your want and mess: Jesus' life is evidence enough that he can handle it.

LESSON 48

On forgiveness

Make allowance for each other's faults, and forgive anyone who offends you. Remember, the Lord forgave you, so you must forgive others.

—Colossians 3.13 (NLT)

After the initial shock of our divorce, I made a conscious decision to forgive my ex for all the hurt he had caused me. I'm sure there were things he felt he needed to forgive me for too, but only the forgiveness I could offer was in my control; I knew it was the best option. But it was only recently, when a relatively new friend asked what happened with the two of us, that I realized I truly had forgiven him. The law requires that anyone wanting to end a marriage due to 'irreconcilable differences' must cite specific reasons. My friend asked me what Fish had cited, and I told her the only one I remember. He claimed that I had wanted a child but that he hadn't been ready or hadn't wanted one. We had a huge row about using that reason, since our much-wanted daughter was not long dead. My friend stared at me open-mouthed when I explained that when I finally told him that if he wanted a divorce, I wanted nothing more to do with him, he had called me 'angry and bitter'. In many ways her quite common viewpoint was prohibiting her from understanding my decision to forgive him. And yet, in Chapter 3 of the book of Colossians, the Apostle Paul talks about living a 'new life'. He urged believers in Colossae to think differently from the way of the world which often encourages greed and selfishness. He reminded them that the message of Christ might be countercultural to their environment, so they would have to dig deep, remembering what Christ had done for them in dying, to try and live a life that glorified God. There was a time when I felt Fish had completely broken me, but now I know that while I remember what he did, I no longer feel it. In Matthew 6.12, Jesus teaches the disciples to pray, saying, 'and forgive us our sins as we forgive those who sin against us'. You don't get one without doing the other. I don't know if you have ever felt this way, as though the bruises from heart-break seem as though they will never truly go away, but the Bible makes it clear that unforgiveness just makes it worse. If we actively withhold forgiveness from someone, it puts a barrier between ourselves and the forgiveness God offers to us every single day.

LESSON 49

Love, honour, respect

As you enter the house of God, keep your ears open and your mouth shut. It is evil to make mindless offerings to God. Don't make rash promises, and don't be hasty in bringing matters before God. After all, God is in heaven, and you are here on earth. So let your words be few.

Too much activity gives you restless dreams; too many words make you a fool.

When you make a promise to God, don't delay in following through, for God takes no pleasure in fools. Keep all the promises you make to him. It is better to say nothing than to make a promise and not keep it.

—Ecclesiastes 5.1–5 (NLT)

I recently attended a wedding where three aspects – love, honour and respect – were cited by the bride's grandfather as key to a successful marriage, reminding us afresh that it's really important to understand these as verbs or 'doing words'. Our relationships are prone to fail when we neglect the art of looking out for and after one another, and this can usually be encapsulated in one of the above magic three. I loved the simplicity and truth in his speech and in the promises made between the happy couple themselves. Personally, I think there's a lot to be said for making your own vows in a relationship, whether that's a marriage or another kind of commitment. Even though you may not have written the words yourself, it is important to actually think about what you're saying or agreeing to. These wise words from King Solomon here in Ecclesiastes that 'it is better to say nothing than to make a promise and not keep it' are in reference to how we approach God and what we say to him in prayer. He advises us not to make rash promises and to 'keep all the promises you make to him,' which sounds obvious because who really wants to piss God off? But for a people-pleaser like me, it is important not just to say what people want to hear, but what you actually plan to stick to. With church-based weddings seen as a commitment with and before God, I think we should treat our wedding vows the same way – a vow made to God and to the other person. I knew a bride who outright refused to include the word 'obey' at her wedding ceremony. Whether or not I disagree, I love that she had pre-read the vows to see whether she could realistically comply with them. One of the greatest gifts we have is choice, so if you're going to make a commitment, like King Solomon suggests, make it one that you can totally get behind, for 'it is better to say nothing than to make a promise and not keep it.'

LESSON 50

Your prince will come

Now Sarai, Abram's wife, had borne him no children. But she had an Egyptian slave named Hagar; so she said to Abram, 'The Lord has kept me from having children. Go, sleep with my slave; perhaps I can build a family through her.'[1]

—Genesis 16.1–2 (NIV)

After my divorce I still had a distinct sense that God's promise to me was for reconciliation. As I searched for God's promises to other believers, I read over the story of Abraham and Sarah – the couple who were promised a son despite both being beyond childbearing age. As they waited, it seemed unlikely to happen naturally, so they got another woman involved, thinking that maybe that was the way God meant for them to have children. At that time, household servants were the property of the owners of the house, so it wouldn't be unusual for a child born to a servant to be brought up by the owners as their own. But their attempts to help God with his plan ended pretty badly with the pregnant servant girl, Hagar, mocking Sarai for her infertility. Ultimately, Hagar's son Ishmael was not the baby God had promised Abraham, and that family line ended up causing huge division in his descendants. Later, Sarai did have a son just as God had promised. If only they'd waited. After reading that, my prayer was specifically that I would not 'birth an Ishmael while waiting for my Isaac'. And this is how God showed me that I needed to keep my

---

1   God changed their names from Abram and Sarai to Abraham and Sarah so I have used both names since they were changed at different points in their story.

eyes fixed on him and not my ex-husband. It has now been six years since the separation and divorce, and I have travelled all over the world, VIP'd my way through two incredible music festivals, met some amazing people, thrown hugely memorable parties, learned to ski, learned to surf, raised money for charity by doing a sky dive, attended the Queen's Garden Party, developed my seriously expensive lingerie habit and laughed a lot. Over those years Fish and I were in and out of contact with each other. He would message me out of the blue saying I had just been on his mind, and I started dreaming about him, something that had never happened when we were actually together. Each time I felt that maybe that would be the point at which we would reconcile. But each time, it was as if God whispered, 'Not yet', and the reminder he gave to Abraham and Sarai of trust and obedience came to mind. I still don't know what God's reconciliation for us looks like, but as I remember this story of Isaac and Ishmael, I'm determined to be present in my every day and not to 'help' God's promise to come to pass in my life. Are you waiting for some sort of reconciliation in your life? If so, I hope this encourages you to wait for God to show you what his best really looks like.

Section Six

Lessons from loss

I was so happy when we found out I was pregnant. My best friend at the time was also pregnant, and so we went round looking at baby stuff together, cooing at anything and everything. Months later, when Annie died a few hours after birth, I felt numb. Then my marriage collapsed.

I was angry at God for allowing these things to happen, and I remember screaming out to him in a park one night, demanding a sign that he was with me. Nothing happened, and I returned home feeling exhausted and defeated. But what took place over the next few years was that I was completely embraced by colleagues and friends – cocooned with a love that I now recognize God had his hand in, surrounding me with people who reminded me that I was not alone.

The church I attended as a pre-teen followed a doctrine heavily focused on the Old Testament and God's judgement. When I finally started to read the Bible in full, including the New Testament, I realized how much he loves us and cares when we are hurting. My richest lessons from loss have undoubtedly come from this season of my life, but in this section I have drawn upon scriptures from the New Testament, Psalms and Proverbs where we see people crying out to God in a whole array of circumstances.

The Bible teaches us to 'laugh with those who laugh and weep with those who weep'. This chapter may take us back to a place of weeping, but I want you to see that the lessons from God in this time are deep and long-lasting and ultimately filled with hope for us all.

LESSON 51

Lessons from my first time

Restore to me the joy of your salvation,
 and make me willing to obey you.
Then I will teach your ways to rebels,
 and they will return to you.
Forgive me for shedding blood, O God who saves;
 then I will joyfully sing of your forgiveness.
Unseal my lips, O Lord,
 that my mouth may praise you.

—Psalm 51.12–15 (NLT)

My mum had a strict 'no sex before marriage and especially not under my roof' rule for myself and my siblings, so I waited . . . until university. I knew back then how valuable my virginity was supposed to be, but I was curious about sex and I wanted to act on those desires. For the first few weeks, my new boyfriend and I would lie side by side in my single bed and do everything except penetrative sex. I knew I was playing with fire because we were both very ready to sleep together, but the guilt I felt stopped me. I was half asleep when it finally happened; he moved so quickly I hardly had time to register anything except to gasp when I realized he was inside me. I didn't stop him or say anything until afterwards; in shock, I said 'I wasn't ready'. Even though I was present in all my sex education classes, I still didn't argue when, as I kicked off at him for not using a condom, he informed me that you can't get pregnant from your first time. David wrote this psalm after he forced Bathsheba to sleep with him and consequently got her pregnant. He then sent her husband off to war to be killed so he wouldn't find out (read the whole story in 2 Samuel, chapters 11 and 12). The psalm is one of repentance as David appeals to God's loving nature to forgive him despite the evil of which he was guilty. I remember feeling as though something special had been taken from me, and I would never be able to get it back. It wasn't, at this point, about feeling guilty for what I had done; I just felt such a huge sense of loss because I knew losing my virginity that way hadn't been God's best for me. Three months later, when I found out I was pregnant, my partner hit the roof and told me repeatedly that he didn't want my, our baby. He drove me to the clinic and told me I was having an abortion. When we got inside, the nurses looked at us both and made him wait outside while they asked me if I was sure, and I said, 'Yes, we're sure.' I wasn't strong enough to say no. When they told me it was over, that powerful sense of loss came over me again. I felt unable to grieve for something that was my fault, and it is only as I write this that I can see the words of this scripture come to life in mine. I'm sure this is not a unique story, and you may know someone who has gone through this experience – or you may have experienced it yourself – and there can be an awful lot of shame around the topic of non-marital sex and abortions. But the lesson I learned here is that God restores, God forgives and he unseals our hushed mouths to praise him. If you find yourself in this situation, I urge you to not stop talking to others and to God. He's got you and he won't let you go.

LESSON 52

Barely there

Give all your worries and cares to God, for he cares about you.
—1 Peter 5.7 (NLT)

In my final year of university, I suffered from what my friend terms 'functional depression'. This refers to a state of being under which, despite suffering from internal trauma, you can operate without alluding to a state of instability. Sometimes I was so used to the feeling of unease, I didn't even realize it was happening. Have you ever felt like that? When there's a part of you that feels like, 'okay, well this is crap', and then another part is like, 'oh yeah, you're right, it is – oh well'. This 'functionality' can often seem like a gift, protecting us from the reality which might otherwise completely overwhelm us. But it also means we continue in a state of falsehood, telling us that we're okay when really what we need to be doing is crying out for help so that someone can hear us and respond. During that year – Easter weekend, to be specific – I found myself alone in the house I shared with two friends. Everyone else had gone home for the weekend, but since the pregnancy shame of my first year, I avoided home as much as possible and always found somewhere else to be. But this time, I had nowhere to run to. 'Give all your worries and cares to God, for he cares for you' is the simple message Peter shared with the Jewish Christians of that time, and it was apt for me too, two years after my first sexual experience had led to the blotting out of the innocent life growing inside me. I was still carrying the pain which had turned to guilt and separated me from God. That weekend, for some reason, even though I wasn't going to church at all at that time, I decided

I would do a three-day fast – from all food, screens and forms of technology. I had fasted before but never by choice since my whole experience of faith up until that point was via someone else's direction. I hardly left my room as I cried out to God, read the Bible and wrote down everything I felt had separated me from God. At the end of those three days, I ripped up the paper containing all the evidence of my sin, both public and private, and I felt his complete peace. I had nothing to prove it, but I knew God had been with me. As I write this now, I'm reminded of that Easter weekend so long ago when Jesus hung upon the cross for all our sins, and then the ripping of the curtain as he died and what separated us from God was destroyed. I still have so much to learn about Jesus but back then, 20-year-old me felt closer to him than I had ever been before. You may be able to identify with this or you may not, but if you have ever felt shame, please know just how much God cares about you and believe that he will lift that shame from you as you pour out your heart directly to him.

LESSON 53

Losing Annie

Yea, though I walk through the valley of the shadow of death,
I will fear no evil: for thou art with me;
thy rod and thy staff they comfort me.

—Psalm 23.4 (KJV)

Sometimes I feel guilty when I think of Annie as my first child. After all, I did get pregnant when I was 18, but Annie was conceived in a loving marriage and, I suppose, in that strange way that we use the term 'foetus' when the child is wanted and an 'unwanted pregnancy' when she is not, Annie was the one we had hoped and prayed for. We had been trying for about a year, and before long I was that person sending pictures of a wee-stained test stick to all my friends. My husband, Fish, was elated; we both were. But I bled through my pregnancy, and although I looked well, I was often sick and would frequently clutch my lower abdomen in pain during the lengthy commute to work. I went to hospital a few times but was always dismissed. When I gave birth to Annie via spontaneous labour – labour that begins and continues without outside intervention – I was on my own after being rushed to hospital from work with excessive bleeding. Our beautiful baby girl slipped out a silent, tiny bundle of limbs. As I tried to catch a glimpse of her, I saw them putting her into a bag, and I wanted to scream out, 'please don't throw my baby away!' But they were just keeping her warm, keeping her alive. I learned the KJV of Psalm 23 as a child so the words seem strong and solid to me in that translation. My experience felt exactly like the 'valley of the shadow of death' mentioned in this scripture. Everything seemed dark and gloomy in those hours following Annie's birth, but I felt God's comfort in odd things like the words of the obstetrician who said, 'Keep praying but remember, if she dies, it is within God's will'. That felt like the 'rod' of comfort: the no-nonsense words preparing me for the outcome. Later, the hospital chaplain prayed over Fish and me as we held Annie's still body, and this was the 'staff' of comfort, the gentle presence of God for us to lean on. In my early stages of pregnancy, I had a dream that something terrible was going to happen, but a strong sense that I would be all right – and I *am* all right because God has made me so. The scripture here is about leaving behind fear. Life can be pretty rubbish, and I know people with much worse stories than mine. But when you believe and trust God to be the shepherd guiding you through the inevitable valleys, he will always find ways to comfort you.

LESSON 54

Unhappy people

When God's people are in need, be ready to help them. Always
be eager to practice hospitality.

—Romans 12.13 (NLT)

Losing my daughter to an early death and my husband to divorce,
one after the other, left me pretty miserable to be around. In the earlier days I hid it with partying, but as I went through the stages of
grief, it became more obvious how unhappy I was. I now wanted to
leave what had once been my dream job but just felt so stuck. I had
completely lost my sense of purpose. These were all the emotions
I was feeling inside, but on the outside, I just seemed really angry
– at everything and everyone. My relationship with my family had
never really healed after I chose to push ahead with the marriage,
and I often felt on the edge of community, but the deployment of
this scripture in practice was a powerful force of support during this
time. I had always been lucky with the people I worked for, but one
of my line managers was particularly caring. I remember going into
her office one day during this period and she looked at me and said,
'Someone needs to take care of you.' And no one was, so she took
up the mantle herself; my workplace became the safest place I had.
She put me forward for training to take my mind off my feeling of
stagnation; she was patient with me when I kicked off about things I
felt were unfair, and she stood up for every business idea I had – not
necessarily because they were good ones, but because she wanted me
to know that she was for me. She was always ready, as it says here, to
help me when I was in need, and I could see her pride when she saw

me through to the other side. No one could have known how deeply hurt I was really feeling, but even if we don't, let's not assume that people are mean for no reason. These days, if we see someone whose anger seems irrational, this scripture in Romans calls us out to help them and be 'eager to practice hospitality.' Sure, we all have our own problems, but they might just be trying to get through a really hard day, and it's possible that God wants to use us to help them.

LESSON 55

Be childlike

When Jesus saw what was happening, he was angry with his disciples. He said to them, 'Let the children come to me. Don't stop them! For the Kingdom of God belongs to those who are like these children. I tell you the truth, anyone who doesn't receive the Kingdom of God like a child will never enter it.'

—Mark 10.14–15 (NLT)

Lorna Byrne, the author of bestseller *Angels In My Hair*, says that she has been seeing and talking with angels since she was a child. Written off as 'retarded' as a young girl, her revelations were mostly ignored, but she continues to see angels in adulthood with a demeanour described by those who meet her as 'childlike'. Children are so sensitive and can sense things that I think we lose touch with as adults. Do you ever feel a subtle nudge to do something which seems slightly bonkers so you ignore it? Or if it involves approaching someone else, we might be afraid of his or her reaction. During Jesus' time on earth, children were not considered of any great importance, so when some parents brought their children to be blessed by Jesus, his disciples shooed them away. Jesus rebuked them for this, explaining how precious they were. When he told them, 'I tell you the truth, anyone who doesn't receive the Kingdom of God like a child will never enter it,' I believe he was talking about the childlike openness and willingness to accept the unknown and unseen without hesitation. Years ago, I was in church not long after our daughter Annie had died. I was feeling particularly broken that morning and sitting behind me was a mother with her 18-month-old baby. I heard her whimpering throughout the opening songs; at that point I could barely look at babies so even though I had always loved children, being near her was difficult. I was about to move when I felt a light tapping on my shoulder. I ignored it, thinking someone had just brushed past me, but then it came again, more persistently this time. I turned around, slightly irritated, to see this beautiful child holding her arms out to me. Her mum looked as surprised as I was and mouthed, 'Do you want to hold her?' For reasons I couldn't fathom, I said yes, and as soon as I took her into my arms, she lay her head down on my shoulder, put her thumb in her mouth and went to sleep. I held her for most of the service, and she was completely silent. Her presence calmed me, and I started to feel the tightening in my stomach loosen as I let waves of affection flow for her. The next time I saw her she wasn't at all interested in me, but I was a lot better by then and recognized that she had answered the Spirit's call to do something. If the Holy Spirit had told her mum to offer me her child to hold, knowing I had just lost a child, she would probably have dismissed the thought. But it was just what I needed to help me on that journey, which would begin the healing in my own heart. It's a hard call, with so many apps, notifications and emails demanding our time and energy, but God's healing through us can be fulfilled if we can learn to be responsive to the Holy Spirit's voice, just like this little girl whose name just happened to be Angel.

LESSON 56

Stay soft

If your gift is to encourage others, be encouraging. If it is giving, give generously. If God has given you leadership ability, take the responsibility seriously. And if you have a gift for showing kindness to others, do it gladly.

—Romans 12.8 (NLT)

Seeing people who have what you have just lost can be brutal, and after Annie died, I seemed to see pregnant women everywhere. One day I saw a pregnant woman on the train, and before I could turn away in sadness, I felt a nudge to pray for her. It seemed ridiculous, and I genuinely wondered whether God had the right person. But I felt six words come into my head, clear and strong: *God bless you and your baby.* I think I might have cried the first time I said it silently, and after that, every time I saw a pregnant woman I felt the nudge to say it again, so I did. Reading this scripture in Romans in isolation sounds like a nice and kind thing to do – 'If your gift is to encourage others, be encouraging. If it is giving, give generously'– but in my NLT Bible, this chapter is headed with the words 'A Living Sacrifice to God'. I realized that it's all very well being encouraging and kind to others when you're in a good place, but when you're not and you still have to do it – well, then it definitely becomes a sacrifice. My blessing of pregnant women continued until I did it almost without thinking. Once I walked up to a woman in Pret and told her I hoped she had a really safe birth and healthy baby. She looked at me in surprise, but her thanks was so heartfelt I wondered if my words might have meant more than I realized. It's so easy for bitterness to take root when we long for something and don't get it. In this season, God revealed to me my gift, and my obedience was rewarded because praying for strangers helped to keep my heart soft and that's exactly how he wants my heart to be. What does your season look like right now? In my experience it's easy to be outwardly focused when things are going well for us, but not so much when we're lying on the sofa for days at a time, eating leftover Deliveroo. But this could be a time when you have a gift to share with someone else, and refocusing your energy could be the thing that gets you back on your feet.

LESSON 57

'You can't sit with us'

All praise to God, the Father of our Lord Jesus Christ. God is our merciful Father and the source of all comfort. He comforts us in all our troubles so that we can comfort others. When they are troubled, we will be able to give them the same comfort God has given us.

—2 Corinthians 1.3–4 (NLT)

I used to get annoyed with people who told me they knew how I felt losing Annie because they had experienced a miscarriage. I'm ashamed to admit this now, but I felt my loss superseded a miscarriage since Annie was born alive. But I've since realized that these distinct differences still land us in the same pool. There is a huge group of people whose loss is rarely considered, often because people tend not to acknowledge (or be aware of) people's miscarriages or because people often go on to have other children so they are presumed to have 'gotten over' an earlier baby loss. This is why we each know little of how the other is suffering, often in silence, because the lack of freedom to share can often keep us in our own private hell. The book of 2 Corinthians is Paul's second letter to this particular group of people, and some discord among them meant he had to try and rally them together and remind them they were all on the same side. In reading this, I was reminded of the truth in the words in this scripture, 'He comforts us in all our troubles so that we can comfort others. When they are troubled, we will be able to give them the same comfort God has given us.' When I publicly shared our loss, both friends and strangers poured out their hearts with their own silent grief, and two close friends told me recently that it wasn't until they experienced their own baby loss that they had a glimpse of my pain. This oft-quoted Mean Girls phrase, 'You can't sit with us', is about everyone else being excluded from a clique requiring a certain je ne sais quoi to be eligible. With baby loss, you're part of a 'clique' that you never asked nor wanted to join. But there is comfort in that glimpse of understanding how the other feels. My relationships with those two friends got much better once they understood and forgave the seemingly erratic behaviour I had portrayed in the wake of Annie's death. They understood why I couldn't go to baby showers or why I sometimes cried when people told me they were pregnant. Being further along in the journey meant I was able to offer support in a different way because while I was no longer in active mourning, I had experienced the stages they were going through. If you're in a position where you 'can't sit with us', I hope you don't feel shut out. It can be hard being a friend to someone going through this, and in my experience the best thing you can do is just be sincere. If you feel you can support, great! If not, that's ok too; just being honest with your friend will help you both understand where you're coming from.

LESSON 58

How death lost its sting

God blesses those who mourn,
for they will be comforted.

—Matthew 5.4 (NLT)

Last year I, along with most of my colleagues, attended the funeral of another colleague who had died having been diagnosed with cancer for a second time. There was immense sadness at the unfairness of this loss of life and for the people left behind – a much-loved husband and teenage daughter. Her favourite piece of music was played in the middle of the ceremony, something she had chosen personally, requesting that the whole ten minutes be heard without interruption. The entire composition was music with no words, and it was in that absence of words that I suddenly had a vision of my colleague, no longer in pain, playing with the little boy she told me she miscarried before he could see this life. And I saw her turn to me and reveal the hand of the little girl she was holding – and I knew it was Annie. I started to cry then, not sad tears but tears of remembrance. I called to memory every conversation we had shared about our lost little ones and of the pain we understood in each other. This scripture is part of a section we know as The Beatitudes, a sermon Jesus taught from up on the side of a mountain. He taught them about the blessings of God, and one of these was this passage in verse 4: 'God blesses those who mourn, for they will be comforted.' God showed me his comfort as I saw my colleague – *his* child – with him and *my* child with him also. Later that evening I thought back to another kind of death, this time the death of the woman I was before my child and the love of my husband had been taken from me. I cried at the memory of my brokenness and every hurt and every pain that had managed to seep its way into my life. I cried for her and for the future she didn't know existed and for the darkness that had threatened to engulf her entire being. When people die, we often say things like, 'they're in a better place now.' I believe that, because I'm a Christian, but I also believe God knows that doesn't necessarily make it easier to let go. He promises we will be comforted whether that comfort comes from close friends or family, revelation, visions or maybe even just a sense of peace. And my prayer for anyone in mourning is that you will experience this blessing from God.

LESSON 59

Letting go of idols

Dear children, keep away from anything that might take God's place in your hearts.

—1 John 5.21 (NLT)

Growing up, my main focus was on having children. I didn't want to be a single mum, but children were definitely higher than marriage on my priority list; this often feels like something celebrated to the point of idolatry in the Church. Whenever I think about idols, I think of the Israelites in Exodus (Chapter 32) where they wanted something to worship so they built a calf-shaped statue made of solid gold. The idols I see around me are famous people, our careers or the money we make, and I try to stay clear of worshipping or making gods out of those things. But recently I heard idolatry defined as this: anything more fundamental than God to your self-worth, significance or value. And as I wrote that down, I suddenly thought, what if having children was my idol? What if I was holding onto that as my *thing*, the thing that consumed me more than anything else? 1 John is an eponymous book of the Bible written by the Apostle John to encourage believers he addresses as 'Dear children', showing his deep love for them as he gives practical instruction for Christian living. When I read this scripture, I thought about how you usually sign off the end of a letter with the most important and pressing piece of information you want to impart so that it doesn't get forgotten. In this letter those last words are 'Dear children, keep away from anything that might take God's place in your hearts.' In the Greek it reads 'keep yourselves from idols.' I used to say I would rather die than not have children. It scared me to think that this deep need may have been weighing me down and directing many a thought, action or decision – perhaps to my detriment. So I've had to let go. And you know what? Maybe I won't have children, or maybe I will; I don't know my future, but for now I feel like I need to know that I will be all right if I don't because God is enough. He really is. If you're at a similar life stage, this might be tough reading. It is for me too, but God really does know how to get us to live our best lives whether that involves children or not; we just have to put him first and trust him.

LESSON 60

Not my will but yours

Shadrach, Meshach and Abednego replied to him, 'King Nebuchadnezzar, we do not need to defend ourselves before you in this matter. If we are thrown into the blazing furnace, the God we serve is able to deliver us from it, and he will deliver us from Your Majesty's hand. But even if he does not, we want you to know, Your Majesty, that we will not serve your gods or worship the image of gold you have set up.'

—Daniel 3.16–18 (NIV)

Have you ever doubted God's goodness? I know I have. From the depths of loss I wondered why He didn't bring back my husband and help us have another child. When it came to God looking out for me, it seemed inconsistent, like sometimes he does, and sometimes he doesn't. When I run into difficulty, the preferred outcome is usually obvious to me – fix it. But then I came across some scriptures which really challenged my level of faith. The book of Daniel is the story of the young men who had been taken to the palace of King Nebuchadnezzar when he took Judah captive. We are not given much insight as to their lives pre-captivity, but these were noblemen, taken from the highest ranking families of Judah to serve in the palace of a king who worshipped other gods – something they knew that God had strictly forbidden (Exod. 34.14). Having passed their training, four of these men had been serving in the palace for some time in high positions when King Nebuchadnezzar had a huge gold statue built and sent round a decree demanding that at the sound of an instrument, everyone must bow down to it. We're not told what Daniel/

Belteshazzar did, but the other three refused and were hauled before the king to explain themselves, with threats to throw them into the furnace if they didn't comply. Reading these four words in their reply in Daniel 3.16–18 actually baffled me: 'even if he does not...' I've spent years getting to know the all-powerful God we serve and how much he loves us and works things out for our good (Rom. 8.28), but this reply showed me that these guys were on a completely different level of faith. They trusted God so implicitly that they didn't even pre-empt what looked like a positive outcome – being saved from the pit. Ultimately, God does save them, which is what we would expect from a loving God, right? Compare this to the cry of Jesus in Mark 14.36, 'Abba, Father', he said, 'everything is possible for you. Take this cup from me. Yet not what I will, but what you will.' What Jesus was about to go through was torturous, just like the three men in Daniel, but God doesn't seem to answer Jesus' prayer. We are privileged to know that both outcomes gave God glory and all men were ultimately rewarded for their faith, but it would have looked very different at the time. These lessons on loss have shown me that God has been working things out for me, as he does for all of us. But honestly, would I have preferred not to have gone through the pain and heartache? One hundred per cent. But we get to a very new level of faith when we can cry out to God for something without relying on his answer to prove himself; when we can say with all honesty, 'not what I will, but what you will.'

Section Seven

Lessons from identity

When I was younger, I would adopt different personas depending on where I was and to whom I was talking. I would even make up new names for myself to match each of these versions of me – I was used to labelling myself just to fit in. My identity shifted with each label.

Recently, I was filling in an application form for my new bank and felt conflicted when asked about my title. Mrs was for wives and I was no longer a wife; Miss felt like a young girl's title and Ms just seemed to scream 'DIVORCED!' So I did what any normal person would do and bought a title, which means I can now use 'Lady' – although, when I finally got my card, it didn't have my title on it anyway so what was the point? Even now, well into my thirties, I struggle – as many do – with my sense of identity.

John 1.12 reads, 'But to all who believed him and accepted him, he gave the right to become children of God' (NIV). This means God has given us a way to identify ourselves which is not dependent on circumstances – not a relationship, our place of birth or our financial status. I don't know what that looks like for you, but I find this assurance freeing. It does away with the need for typecasting as Christians. If we accept God, we are his heirs and we can be whoever we want within that identity, whether that's a Miss, a Ms, a Mrs or even a Lady. Our true identity can be found in him.

LESSON 61

Why I'm not here for religion

There is no fear in love. But perfect love drives out fear, because fear has to do with punishment. The one who fears is not made perfect in love.

—1 John 4.18 (NIV)

The word religion is often described as a particular system of faith and worship. This is the kind of religion I grew up on, ultimately involving trying to make myself acceptable to God. I thought I needed to prove myself in order to be loved by him; I couldn't identify with a love that required absolutely nothing from me. This was influenced by the many, many rules and laws that God gave to the Israelites in the Old Testament in order to be considered holy – which are pretty exhausting. 'Indeed, there is no one on earth who is righteous, no one who does what is right and never sins' (Eccles. 7.20), meaning sacrifices had to be paid to atone for these sins. There was a sense of fear in not obeying the commandments, with the sacrifices necessary to 'make peace' with God. But this scripture in 1 John 4.18 says that 'perfect love drives out fear, because fear has to do with punishment,' and Jesus himself took the punishment of sin that we could not conquer no matter how many sacrifices we might make (Isa. 53.5). When Jesus breathed his last breath, Matthew 27.51 reports that the curtain in the temple, which separated those who came to worship God from the inner 'holy place', was completely torn top to bottom – representative of what Jesus came to do. Reading about the life of Jesus, I can see how everything he did was out of love: strong, unwavering, unconditional love. He loved and forgave those who wanted him killed (Luke 23.34) and because of the love he had for all people, he spent more time with those in need than anyone else as an example of how we should be (Luke 10.30–37). When asked to name the greatest commandment, Jesus replied, "'Love the Lord your God with all your heart and with all your soul and with all your mind." This is the first and greatest commandment. And the second is like it: "Love your neighbour as yourself."' Religion commands us to do something for fear of the repercussions if we don't. The day I realized that God loves me unconditionally was life-changing, because that fear was removed and replaced with relationship. In my experience, Religion = Fear, but Jesus = Love, and it's Jesus in Christianity that I think needs to shine more. What do you say when people ask if you're religious?

LESSON 62

Why I had to leave church to find God

For I am convinced that neither death nor life, neither angels nor demons, neither the present nor the future, nor any powers, neither height nor depth, nor anything else in all creation, will be able to separate us from the love of God that is in Christ Jesus our Lord.

—Romans 8.38–39 (NIV)

I think I was about five when we first started going to church, and I was baptized by choice when I was 16. I was in the youth group, the choir and helped out at the church crèche. After university I joined a Christian women's group, started dating a Christian and spent most of my time with Christian friends. Living in my Christian bubble, it seemed God was everywhere but I didn't really know him. In this scripture from Romans, Paul says that Jesus embodies that love that God has for us and that nothing 'will be able to separate us from the love of God that is in Christ Jesus our Lord.' At some point I sensed that I had only experienced a glimpse of that love, and I wanted more. I loved my church life and church family, but most of my time was spent doing all the stuff that embodied the look of a believer and less of the receiving from God. In church I relied solely on someone else to teach me about him and while it worked for a while, ultimately, it was like using a middle man to have a relationship. Once I understood that, I made a drastic decision to spend the following 12 months without stepping into a traditional church other than what actually did end up being four weddings and a funeral. I set aside time in the mornings to read my Bible, pray and then meditate to give me head space to hear from God. Previously, in all my doing of the 'God stuff', I hadn't understood that ultimately God wants us to know that he can talk to us directly, not only through a prophet or revelation from someone else. I learned that unless we seek him for ourselves, we don't really have a relationship with him, and he wants one. Years ago I came across a brand called 'Jesus Loves Me'. It was plastered all over t-shirts, jumpers and caps, and I remember thinking it was a bit self-interested. Shouldn't Christians be walking around telling people that Jesus loves them? It wasn't until my Gap Year with God that I realized the truth that all that we are and can be as Christians rests in us knowing with our entire being that God loves us, and it is from that certainty that everything else unfolds (1 John 4.16). My non-Christian friends found it weird that I was still calling myself a Christian while not actually going to church, and my Christian friends were concerned I was losing my faith. Spending time out of church is not for everyone, but spending time with God is, as is sharing time in community, and doing so has helped me build a solid foundation for my relationship with him and from that, my relationship with others. Indeed, our concept of what 'church' is can sometimes be too linked to a building, organization or traditions instead of a community of believers. This 'Gap Year with God' might look very different to you – and I'm not advocating everyone stops going to church – but honestly, if we don't know God loves us, how can we ever share his love with someone else?

LESSON 63

Embrace your inner outlier

> But his brothers hated Joseph because their father loved him more than the rest of them. They couldn't say a kind word to him.
>
> —Genesis 37.4 (NLT)

How do you respond when asked to identify yourself? Do you talk about where you were born? Where your parents are from? Your career? Your relationship status? I always felt like a voyeur growing up; I remember looking around to make sure I 'fit in' wherever I found myself. I'm the child of Nigerian-born expats – they bought their first home here in the early 1980s, and I was born and grew up just outside of London. While we ate Nigerian food at home and had Nigerian friends, my parents said they decided not to teach us any of their languages since they were from different tribes and didn't want to 'cause confusion'. I have also, at the time of writing, never stepped foot on the land of my heritage, something which has always left me feeling slightly like an outlier in certain group settings. I just want to 'belong'. Joseph was a clear outlier in his family. His brothers hated him and his mother was dead. Even if you read the full story of Joseph in Genesis (Chapters 37–50) and you think (as I did) he sounds like a cocky kid telling his family that one day he would rule over them, being his father Jacob's favourite ultimately wasn't his fault. Joseph's mother, Rachel, was Jacob's favourite wife, and so he was a much longed-for child, while his brothers were born to two maids and Leah, who Jacob was tricked into marrying (Gen. 29.16–30). As a result, Joseph was resented by his brothers, ignored and seemed to spend most of his time alone. What Joseph didn't know at the time but had hints of in his dreams was that God had a bigger plan for him that would propel his status from outlier to the glue that enabled his family to stay alive and together ('It was God who sent me here ahead of you to preserve your lives.' Gen. 45.5b). When I found myself one of only a handful of black students among mostly Jews at a Church of England private school; when told 'you sound white' by members of the African and Caribbean society at university; when people at church ask if I'm married and/or have children – the clang of outlier has rung loud in my ears. But just like Joseph, I am God's favourite too (and weird as it might be to comprehend, we all are because if not, John 3.16 seems a pretty high price to pay for people you're just 'meh' about). Does any of this ring true for you? If so, take solace in that while our outlier status might feel difficult now, one day it might be the very thing that propels us to a future of being the 'glue' between the different groups of people we have worried about fitting in with.

LESSON 64

Understanding privilege

So in Christ Jesus you are all children of God through faith, for all of you who were baptized into Christ have clothed yourselves with Christ. There is neither Jew nor Gentile, neither slave nor free, nor is there male and female, for you are all one in Christ Jesus. If you belong to Christ, then you are Abraham's seed, and heirs according to the promise.

—Galatians 3.26–29 (NIV)

Privilege finds itself in many forms, and social media introduces me to new ones all the time. There is white privilege, male privilege, skinny privilege, pretty privilege, British privilege, socio-economic privilege and the list continues. Privilege relates to the dominative power working within all facets of society and has recently been causing serious unrest as people open up about how it has negatively affected them. Ultimately the privilege or lack of privilege is linked to our sense of identity, and if I'm honest, sometimes being a black woman can feel like being at the bottom of the proverbial food chain. But this changes if I consider what has been described as an invisible package of unearned assets: I'm slim, was born in Britain and went to private school. This gives me 'privileges' such as not having to worry about fitting into a seat on public transport, having little to zero issues accessing a visa when travelling and knowing how to wield a lacrosse stick. In this scripture Paul talks about 'Jewish privilege' whereby the Jews of that time, who were descendants of Abraham, knew that they had been called as God's chosen people ('for you are a people holy to the Lord your God. Out of all the peoples on the face

of the earth, the Lord has chosen you to be his treasured possession.'
Deut. 14.2), and there was a tendency for them to view themselves as
superior to others. In Galatians, Paul was writing because a group of
Jewish believers had told Gentile (non-Jewish) Christians that they
had to submit to the laws of Moses in order to be saved. Paul writes
to remind them that we are saved by submission to and relationship
with God and not by any other means: 'There is neither Jew nor Gentile, neither slave nor free, nor is there male and female, for you are
all one in Christ Jesus…' This promise outlined in Romans 10.9–13
is evidence of God smashing privilege – giving us all access from an
even playing field and an identity we can all connect with. So while
it isn't helpful to pretend we are not privileged in some way or other,
we can stop using it as an identifier because God has called us to be
one in Jesus Christ.

LESSON 65

Who am I?

Jesus answered, 'I am the way and the truth and the life. No one comes to the Father except through me.'

—John 14.6 (NIV)

Who am I? It's such an existential question, and not one you want to reply to lightly. When I was still in primary school, a perceptive teacher gave me this advice: 'Show me your friends and I'll show you who you are' – and I've never forgotten it. I'd finally gotten in with the popular kids in class, but my teacher could see I was changing, and not for the better. Recently, I was at a neighbour's dinner party and found myself repeatedly asked, 'What do you do?' It's an innocent enough question but one I feel is almost certainly (intrinsically) linked to another: 'Who are you?' And no matter how much I love my job, it never seems to match up with who I really am. In stark contrast, Jesus is confident: 'I am the way, the truth and the life. No one comes to the Father except through me.' Jesus' life on earth was the epitome of his purpose. He healed and he loved. At the end of Exodus 15.26, God says, 'I am the Lord who heals you.' In 1 John 4.8 we read, 'Whoever does not know love does not know God, because God is love.' Undoubtedly, Jesus is who he says he is. Jesus knew exactly why he was here, and he fulfilled his purpose here on earth in keeping with that. As a child, he disappeared during a family trip and spent time talking with religious leaders in the temple. When he is reprimanded for causing his parents to worry, Jesus says in Luke 2.49, 'Why were you searching for me? . . . Didn't you know I had to be in my Father's house?' He was really saying,

'Don't you know why I am here? Don't you know who I am?' But we read in verse 51, 'Then he went down to Nazareth with them and was obedient to them.' He fit in his 'why' with his current situation. Could Jesus have started healing and teaching at age 12 as he was at this point? Maybe, but we read in verse 52 that he manages to fulfil his purpose right where he is – as a child, obedient to his parents: 'Jesus grew in wisdom and stature, and in favour with God and man.' The modern desire for self-discovery runs deep. We look for more meaning in our everyday lives, and we travel in order to 'find ourselves'. Maybe we are in too much of a hurry to define ourselves by what's going on around us – things like who our friends are and what we do to make money. Jesus' example teaches us that we can have a strong sense of why we are here and who we are, even if on the outside it just looks like business as usual. As we read the Bible and spend time trying to listen to God in quiet moments, I believe he reveals to us our individual 'whys' because we know that he hears and answers our prayers (1 John 5.15). And it might be that we have a big life and job change, or we might not. But since a life with God is more often than not about what we do right where we are, the answer might be simpler than we think.

LESSON 66

Wilderness years

And the child grew and became strong in spirit; and he lived in the wilderness until he appeared publicly to Israel.

—Luke 1.80 (NIV)

For years, what I did was not what I felt my purpose was, but since I was still to identify that purpose, I felt stuck between a rock and a confusing place, a wilderness. John the Baptist had a very clear purpose from when he was a child, with these words in Luke 1.14–17 (NIV) spoken to his father, Zachariah, by an angel before he was even born:

He will be a joy and delight to you, and many will rejoice because of his birth, for he will be great in the sight of the Lord. He is never to take wine or other fermented drink, and he will be filled with the Holy Spirit even before he is born. He will bring back many of the people of Israel to the Lord their God. And he will go on before the Lord, in the spirit and power of Elijah, to turn the hearts of the parents to their children and the disobedient to the wisdom of the righteous—to make ready a people prepared for the Lord.

John's purpose was set, but it's interesting that even though his father was a priest (Luke 1.5), he didn't spend his 'training time' in the temple; he spent it alone, in the wilderness. And he isn't the only person in the Bible who experiences this; in Matthew 4, Jesus is 'led by the Spirit into the wilderness to be tempted by the devil.' And like John, it is only after that that Jesus begins his ministry. Similarly,

Joseph went through a kind of wilderness when he was sold as a slave and imprisoned for years before his visions were finally realized (Gen. 37–41). While feelings of loneliness and doubt might come into play in the wilderness, whatever that might look like, it is also a place to become self-aware, to know what we are made of and to have our beliefs and ideals tested. It is a place to be made stronger so that we emerge with unshakeable trust and confidence in God and his ability to work through us. A wilderness is dictionary-defined as an uncultivated, uninhabited and inhospitable region, a neglected or abandoned area. But a wilderness is also a natural environment on earth that has not been significantly modified by human activity. What better place to hear and learn from God? Say, for example, you feel your purpose is to be a wife, but you feel like you've been single forever. Maybe your years of singleness and finding out what makes you tick are preparing you to pick the right person for your future? Or maybe you really want to start your own business, but you feel stuck in a job with the worst colleagues. That could also be God's way of preparing you to deal with all kinds of people before you launch out on your own. I suppose the lesson here for all of us is don't despise the wilderness; it could just provide the survival skills you never knew you needed.

LESSON 67

Fighting fear

For God has not given us a spirit of fear and timidity, but of power, love, and self-discipline.

—2 Timothy 1.7 (NLT)

I was about seven when we moved to a new house, and on the day we arrived Mum sent my siblings and me off to the newsagent round the corner with a pound each. When we got to the large sweets section, salivating with excitement, I suddenly felt overwhelmed with all the different options. That £1 went much further back then, and I wasn't sure whether I should get more sugared jelly hearts or whether I would like the taste of the plain cola bottles. I didn't realize how long we had been debating until I heard my mother's voice from the doorway, angry with worry because as it turned out, we had been gone for almost an hour. As I got older, I continued to struggle with decision-making – which university to attend, what groceries to buy, what to put on the front covers of the magazine I edited. What would people think of me in the admissions office, at the cash registers and in board meetings? What would my choices reveal about my identity? This scripture in 2 Timothy was from a letter written from prison by the Apostle Paul to his friend Timothy, giving testimony of God's faithfulness and his complete trust in him. His strong words, 'For God has not given us a spirit of fear and timidity, but of power, love and self-discipline' encourage Timothy to stand firm for what he believes to be right as he goes on to say 'So never be ashamed to tell others about our Lord.' It seems a weird thing to acknowledge now, but when I read these words, I realized that I hadn't seen my indecision as *fear*. I just thought I took longer than most other people to settle on something. But God showed me that I was fearful, and that was not the type of spirit he has deposited in – or one he wants for – his children. I was fearful because I wasn't secure in my identity, and as ridiculous as it is, I worried that I would be exposed somehow. Self-belief or self-confidence is an assurance in one's personal judgement, ability and/or power and is exhorted in most, if not all, societies. But God hasn't called us to rely on ourselves and our own judgement; he has given us his Spirit to guide us: 'I will teach you wisdom's ways and lead you in straight paths' (Proverbs 4.11). As Paul knew well, there is never any guarantee for what a supposed 'good' or 'wrong' decision will lead to, but as we identify with God as our Father and trust him for all things, we can be sure of this scripture in Romans 8.28: 'And we know that in all things God works for the good of those who love him, who[a] have been called according to his purpose.'

LESSON 68

You *are* good enough

Then Mary took about a pint of pure nard, an expensive perfume; she poured it on Jesus' feet and wiped his feet with her hair. And the house was filled with the fragrance of the perfume. But one of his disciples, Judas Iscariot, who was later to betray him, objected.

—John 12.3–4 (NIV)

'It's not you, it's me.' I've never actually said those words, but I have often thought them as I've tried to understand why I've been dumped by exes and failed to receive callbacks on job applications – both occurrences seeming evidence that I have fallen short and don't quite measure up. The spirit of rejection is something I have battled with pretty much my whole life, and the perpetual sound of the door clanging in my face is something that I've really had to push through. If I'm honest, it's one of the reasons I struggled in the modelling industry where ultimately you have to get used to being told you're not good enough ten times in a row and keep going back to castings until you get a 'yes'. For anyone struggling with acceptance and 'fitting in', Jesus is the guy – whether you consider yourself a Christian or not. We read about how he spent time with and helped the weak and the outcasts and paid greater attention to women and children than was considered normal within the culture of the time. Even the men he chose for his disciples were a pretty random mix – including a tax collector and a fisherman – so it's reassuring that this is the kind of God we serve. This scripture comes from John's account of Jesus' time on earth as he was having dinner at the home of a man he had raised from the dead. The dinner was being held in his honour and one of the hosts, Mary, 'took about a pint of pure nard, an expensive perfume; she poured it on Jesus' feet and wiped his feet with her hair. And the house was filled with the fragrance of the perfume.' Judas rebuked her actions, saying to Jesus, 'Why wasn't this perfume sold and the money given to the poor? It was worth a year's wages.' While he may have been correct in his statement, in his objection what he was actually doing was dismissing Mary's gift. Jesus' feet would likely have been dusty and dirty from travelling so by using expensive perfumed oil and her hair (1 Corinthians 11.15), Mary was honouring Jesus with what she had. Verses 7–8 read, '"Leave her alone," Jesus replied. "It was intended that she should save this perfume for the day of my burial. You will always have the poor among you, but you will not always have me."' His reply validates and affirms both Mary and her actions. He even alludes to a sense that Mary is on to something his disciples haven't quite understood – his oncoming death. I can't imagine how Mary must have felt, being so centred in Jesus' bask of love and protection, but it's something I try and remember when I'm feeling sidelined or rejected. The whole world might reject us, but it's imperative to know that when it comes to Jesus, when we give him our all, his response is one of validation and acceptance: 'She's with me.'

LESSON 69

Take me back to Egypt

The Israelites said to them, 'If only we had died by the LORD's hand in Egypt! There we sat round pots of meat and ate all the food we wanted, but you have brought us out into this desert to starve this entire assembly to death.'

—Exodus 16.3 (NIV)

When I was married and visited my single friends, I occasionally thought about how fun it would be if I lived in a London flatshare. Then I found myself divorced and facing that very opportunity (Thanks, God). In my new place I had a huge room with three double wardrobes and an amazing roof terrace with outdoor furniture perfect for al fresco dining. I loved living there, but one day I realized I had had enough of sharing. I was fed up with waiting for others to use the bathroom, picking up after people and not having enough space to cook. I relished my own space, and as I was approaching my sixth year in the house, I was offered the opportunity to have that. I was elated and couldn't wait to start decorating. Then, not long after I moved into my new place, I discovered the roof was leaking. Up until then I had been singing God's praises, but at that point I was like, 'Seriously, Lord?! Why not just leave me back in the flatshare? I didn't have this problem there!' And then almost immediately I recalled this story of the Israelites in Exodus. Oppressed and worked mercilessly as slaves by the Egyptians for 430 years, the Israelites had cried out to be rescued, and God had sent Moses to lead them out of Egypt and into the land he had promised them. They had just seen God work miracles in the plagues he sent on the Egyptians so that Pharaoh would let them go (Exod. 7.14–12.33) and literally make a path for them through the Red Sea away from Pharaoh's army (Exod. 14.21–31), and they had drunk the clean water God had provided for them in the middle of the desert (Exod. 15.22–25). These had been recent miracles, one after the other, and yet just a month after they had left Egypt, they were complaining again, not only were they not trusting God to provide food for them, they also started to complain about how much better their lives had been in bondage, 'There we sat around pots filled with meat and ate all the bread we wanted.' Crazy talk, and yet it struck a chord with me when I thought about how at the first sign of trouble I immediately started wishing myself back in a situation I once couldn't wait to leave. Have you ever really wanted something, like really wanted it – and then started complaining about it once you have it? And it's not really because we're ungrateful; it's just that it might not look like what we expect. Life isn't perfect even when it looks like it should be – when we have what we asked for – but God foresees any obstacles. So the best thing we can do is to remind ourselves in every situation: God's got this.

LESSON 70

Not everyone has to like you

If you belonged to the world, it would love you as its own. As it is, you do not belong to the world, but I have chosen you out of the world.

—John 15.19a (NIV)

As you may have already figured, I hate it if people don't like me. In social situations I usually go out of my way to get to know new people and ingratiate myself with them. I have always applauded myself at this because it seems like a good, a *God,* thing to do, like the Good Samaritan of Social Behaviours. For years I would toe a very thin line at work as I tried to be friends with the people I managed so they'd only say good things about me behind my back. It's easy to have self-imposed expectations of what a Christian should look like, which are based on what the world looks for in a 'good person'. We might think we have to be super nice or liked by everyone. Whether they believe or not, there aren't many adults who don't know about God, but that isn't at all to say that they like him. Even when Jesus was on earth, we know that lots of people didn't like him, taking offence at what he had to say and who he claimed to be and ultimately crucifying him on a cross. In this scripture in John, Jesus explains that when he called them to be his disciples, they moved from becoming people of the world to people of God, and that's the same call we have today. As followers of God, we will face many of the things that he did: unbelief, taunting and persecution. Jesus may have had many followers but he didn't gain them by being, 'nice'. He was simply himself and people liked or disliked him as they chose.

Today there are around eight billion people in the world, and I'm never going to be friends with all of them. God has not called us to share his word by being people pleasers; he has called us to share his truth – in love, yes, but in truth – and that means some people won't like us. It may be daunting to think like that, but we know that Jesus experienced the same thing, and since life is not Facebook, we know we're not here for the 'likes'.

Section Eight

Lessons from dating

It may seem strange having a section on 'Dating' come after the one on 'Marriage' – but that's exactly what happened for me. Dating after divorce has been interesting. First of all, I never knew how much of a turnoff a divorcee is to Christian men. Or at least to the ones with 'LOOKING FOR A PROVERBS 31 WOMAN!' in caps on their Christian dating app profiles. Post-divorce dating was fun at first, as I realized my flirting game was still strong and the excitement of a potential 'winner' seemed a simple click away. But those old feelings of insecurity crept back up, and without the comfort of knowing that there was someone who chose me, I felt pretty exposed. That was an important lesson for me to learn: marriage didn't stop me feeling insecure; it just hid it.

I know that some Christians don't believe in dating, and I'm not here to pass comment on that. For me, personally, I know that there was a time when I was dating and I learned a lot, and there was a time (later) when God told me to stop for a season. This section is about the former, so for the purposes of the next ten lessons, let's take dating to mean: romantic relationships outside of a long-term commitment.

Like many of you (I'm guessing), I've had some great dating experiences and some not-so-great experiences, but for some reason I seem to be someone who learns by doing. So if you're the same, I hope we can enjoy knowing we've not been alone out on that bruised-heart-risking battlefield.

LESSON 71

In love with 'love'

Promise me, O women of Jerusalem,
   by the gazelles and wild deer,
   not to awaken love until the time is right.
                              —Song of Songs 2.7 (NLT)

Someone asked me recently how many times I had been in love. It's an interesting question. I thought I was in love when I was about five. One of my au pairs had a nephew the same age as me who was in a TV commercial. I thought he was wonderful, and we played together and borrowed each other's toys. First love. I thought I was in love when I was 15. My friend's brother was the only guy in our church youth group and went to the same school as my best friend's boyfriend. I figured we would be the type of teenage sweethearts who ended up married with kids. I thought I was in love when I was at university. I met someone who showed me an edgier side to life, and I grew up very quickly in the year or so we were together. I thought I was in love when I was in my early twenties and met someone who on paper was the perfect Adam to my Eve. Without an official engagement, we planned a future together and told everyone that we were destined for each other. And then there was the guy I met a couple of years later, the one I actually got married to. Each break-up (except maybe for five-year-old Tola) felt terribly painful – like a breaking down of my being, which then needed to be rebuilt, slowly and painfully. People often talk about the incredible power of a love relationship, and I really bought into that sense of *falling* into it. I couldn't quite see that there is an element of choice in love which we do have power over.

159

Lessons from dating

This scripture in Song of Songs is a subtle reminder to use wisdom when it comes to romantic love: 'Promise me, O women of Jerusalem, by the gazelles and wild deer, not to awaken love until the time is right.' There is so much we can do to avoid future heartache when we are careful about how and where we place our love for another. My timeline suggests I've been in love plenty, with my eagerness for someone preventing me from seeing any cracks in relationships and getting me lost in what I thought was the all-consuming power of love. When God revealed to me this tendency, it was with a caution that I should guard my heart against anything but the real deal, and it has been my prayer and advice to others ever since. We all crave love, right? But without getting overly spiritual about it, the love we experience with a romantic partner will always be secondary to the love God has for us. To be in love and to be loved is truly wonderful, but God's love is the purest example of it and the only one which will truly satisfy.

It's not what you think

Be humble, thinking of others as better than yourselves.
—Philippians 2.3b (NLT)

Recently I went to a Christian media event and ended up swapping numbers with the only person in the room who wasn't a Christian – though I didn't know that at first. After dating people who didn't share my faith and never finding that common ground, I was now seeking someone who did. With this guy, I was excited to have found someone who looked like the worship leader of my dreams; dark hair, hipster beard, brooding eyes and completely covered in tattoos. From the snatches of text conversation we exchanged before we eventually met up, I began to sense that he wasn't a believer, but at that point I felt too awkward to ask and agreed to meet up anyway just in case I was wrong. A non-Christian friend asked why it was important; wasn't it enough to find a 'good guy'? I struggled to answer and ended up mumbling some rubbish which unfortunately sounded as though I considered Christians a better class of people. In my NLT Bible, this scripture comes from a chapter with the heading: 'Have the attitude of Christ'. And the words Paul wrote to the people of Philippi at the beginning of this letter embody that: 'Be humble, thinking of others as better than yourselves.' It is very easy, when we think about finding a life partner, to begin looking for someone who shares and encourages our faith in well, good faith, but to quickly slip into thinking that a fellow Christian is somehow superior to anyone else. But thinking of ourselves as better is a message Jesus repeatedly eschewed while he was on earth and is echoed in this scripture. On our date I discovered that not only was my hipster not a Christian, but on discovering that I was, his polite but firm rebuttal was 'you're hot and fun to hang out with, but I can't date someone who is a Christian'. And it's funny, because while I had written off men because of their lack of faith before, I had never had someone write me off because of mine. In this situation I recognized God trying to teach me not so much about who I should or shouldn't date, but about humility in my approach to dating. Like me, you may think it's important to share your faith with someone, but Christians are not better than non-Christians. Choosing who you date is one thing, and we will all have our preferences and deal-breakers, but seeing ourselves as belonging to a pool of superheroes in Jesus suits is far from the attitude we see represented in the God we claim to serve.

LESSON 73

Sex = Love?

But Amnon wouldn't listen to her, and since he was stronger than she was, he raped her. Then suddenly Amnon's love turned to hate, and he hated her even more than he had loved her. 'Get out of here!' he snarled at her.

—2 Samuel 13.14–15 (NLT)

Modern Hollywood rom-coms present a narrative in which sex between a couple is often the prelude to a fairy-tale ending: Sex=Love. I had been brought up with 'No sex before marriage' drummed into my head, but in my teens all I could think of was all those films in which sleeping together affirmed a couples' love for each other, questioning and exploring what this might mean for me. Even if they didn't sleep together immediately, it was usually the physical consummation of their relationship which led them to exclaim, 'I love you!' Rarely did I see them declare their love pre-sex. Harry (or at least let's call him that here) was tall, good-looking and most importantly to 19-year-old me, a few years older. At a house party, a well-meaning friend shut us in a cupboard to allow us to talk away from the other girls loitering around him. As she shoved the door closed, I sat on his lap and giggled nervously as we both fell into the rom-com of my dreams. As our eyes adjusted to the dark, he stroked my face and told me how beautiful I was; I told him I liked his smile, and we started kissing. He lifted me up (just like in the films!), placed me on my feet and we left the party holding hands. Back at my shared house, I could feel my heart pounding as he gently undressed me. I felt his desire for me – was this love? But after we had sex, he immediately got dressed and left. In Chapter 13 of 2 Samuel, one of King David's sons, Amnon, tells his adviser, 'I'm in love with Tamar, my brother Absalom's sister' (verse 4), so much so that he becomes physically ill from not being able to 'have her' (verse 2 – the possessive here is the first indicator that his desire might not be the love he claims). So his adviser helps him to engineer a situation where he is able to get Tamar alone. Once he does, he grabs her and says, 'Come to bed with me, my darling sister' (verse 11), but when she refuses, he rapes her and less than four verses later, in verse 15, we read the spine-chilling words, 'Then suddenly Amnon's love turned to hate, and he hated her even more than he had loved her.' How horrifyingly quickly that 'love' changed, something I had experienced when Harry left having fulfilled his desire for me. The burning desire of *want* is not the same as the more considerate *love* that suggests a commitment beyond the physical (1 Corinthians 13.4–7). This scripture also provided the painful lesson that desire can be sated, and it is for our good that God wants us to seek long-lasting connections rather than quick fixes.

LESSON 74

Listen to your gut

Now Abraham moved on from there into the region of the Negev and lived between Kadesh and Shur. For a while he stayed in Gerar, and there Abraham said of his wife Sarah, 'She is my sister.' Then Abimelek king of Gerar sent for Sarah and took her. But God came to Abimelek in a dream one night and said to him, 'You are as good as dead because of the woman you have taken; she is a married woman.'

—Genesis 20.1–3 (NIV)

Sometimes we humans need to learn the same lesson over and over again – and for me no more so than with boys. I met someone on a long train journey who I got on with really well, ordering drinks as we played games together until a technical fault meant that we all had to disembark at a village just outside of our destination. This would normally make me furious, but this time it was an opportunity: we quickly found a pub to continue our conversations, with our conversations once again leading to much more. Our physical encounters (which, I have to admit, were pretty great) continued for a good few months until I started to feel dissatisfied with his lack of commitment and increasingly stagnant conversations. But I couldn't break it off. 'What was the alternative?' I thought at the time – I had had enough of being single and had already invested time and emotion into this relationship. One day when we were together, I suddenly felt overwhelmingly sad, and a voice from deep within me whispered *I don't want to do this anymore*. It was a very clear, sad voice, and I knew it came from the Holy Spirit, articulating what I could not make my physical self comprehend: I wanted out. In this scripture, taken from Genesis 20, we find Abraham lying about his relationship with his wife, instead referring to her as his sister so that he would not attract trouble from the other men wanting to sleep with her. King Abimelek later sends for Sarah as he wants to sleep with her (bizarrely within his cultural rights at the time). Then God intervenes, speaking to Abimelek in a dream and telling him the truth about Sarah's relationship status. Abimelek protests his innocence and God replies, 'Yes, I know you did this with a clear conscience, and so I have kept you from sinning against me. That is why I did not let you touch her.' In my situation, I was the one with the power to stop it, and in Abraham's, the king was – and so God spoke to us in his own way so that we would listen. It was a few more months before I had the courage to break off my own relationship, but I discovered that day that God cares so much about us that he will literally interrupt us right in the middle of our mess to pull us out of it.

LESSON 75

Tell him!

An honest answer is like a kiss of friendship.

—Proverbs 24.26 (NLT)

One year at the music festival Coachella, my friends and I would yell 'Tell him!' at each other whenever one of us mentioned a guy we thought was good-looking. We did it partly because we were all hyped up – it was Coachella, after all – but also to remind us that we *can*. Women are so often used to waiting for the man to make a move, even if we've already decided we're into him. In fact, I've been told quite recently that I should never act too interested if I like someone because men like the chase. And while I get that, I think we need to remember that we have a choice in this whole dating thing. Growing up as a Christian, I heard the word 'picked' quite a lot in dating chat. There was a strong sense that women were prized possessions purely existing to be preened for a future partner, and I really took this to heart. I tried to be as attractive, physically and figuratively, as possible. I would admire boys from afar and only show an interest when someone first showed an interest in me. Proverbs is full of wise, notable sayings, and this verse in Chapter 24 stands out to me as a call to be honest in relationships – friendships or otherwise. Honesty is a virtue extolled throughout the Bible (Prov. 10.9; Eph. 4.25; Col. 3.9) and is important to God and how he wants us to live (Prov. 12.22). I think today's dating scene can sometimes cause us to treat it like a game – how long should we wait before replying to messages so we don't seem too eager? How did our date rate against others based on his choice of restaurant? I know I personally have found it all too easy to hide behind a facade of game, set, match when I really would have preferred the transparency of an honest answer. Being open with our feelings gives us the benefit of starting on an even keel within a partnership and setting the tone for the relationship to come, whether that be a couple of dates or a forever thing. Of course, you're more open to rejection that way, but let's be honest (and that's the point here), an upfront 'thanks but no thanks' from someone you approach is so much better than wasting your precious time playing games, when God needs your full attention for all he has for you.

LESSON 76
Do something

I know that there is nothing better for people than to be happy and to do good while they live. That each of them may eat and drink, and find satisfaction in all their toil – this is the gift of God.

—Ecclesiastes 3.12–13 (NIV)

It was at the 'what now?' stage following the years after my divorce that I began to feel the pressure to meet someone else. To many in the outside world, 'moving on' meant 'moving on to someone new.' I found myself seeking ways to be open to meeting someone, and being a practical person, I found it really frustrating that, while the advice given to help you achieve your life goals is for you to envision them – visualize, mind map, create vision boards, etc. – when it comes to matters of the heart, you're told that it will happen when you least expect it. Sure. The idea conjured up visions of games lessons at school where only the fit and able got picked by the team captains while the others stood staring at the floor, hoping not to be left until last. It was a revelation to discover that 'sitting pretty' is not in keeping with the John 10.10 life I sought to live. Wise King Solomon comes to this conclusion in Ecclesiastes, 'I know that there is nothing better for people than to be happy and to do good while they live.' As he is the one person in the Bible who had made it his mission to seek peace apart from God, only to discover he can't, I take the advice written in this short book quite seriously. The key thing he talks about here is of satisfaction in our work and existence as a 'gift from God.' And so, this scripture in Ecclesiastes reminds me to not see this time so much as a time of waiting, but instead as space to look to what I do have in this season and enjoy using it for his glory, whether that be money, energy or talent. If you feel like you're waiting – and not actively growing in the process – don't just sit around doing nothing. Join a dating app if you feel like that's right for you, or a gym, or a language course – whatever, but do something – and enjoy it! The hardest thing about waiting for something to happen is not knowing exactly when it will happen. So the only way to be happy while you're waiting is to not wait passively, but instead recognize and embrace everything God has put in front of you today.

LESSON 77
Season of Tinder

See what great love the Father has lavished on us, that we should
be called children of God! And that is what we are!

—1 John 3.1a (NIV)

I joined Tinder back when it was just a dating app, not one known
for casual 'hook-ups'. I also joined Guardian Soulmates, Christian Connections and Inner Circle, just to cast my net a bit wider
and increase my chance at catching that fish. Swiping past people's
eager-looking faces on Tinder soon became a game in which my
heart beat faster with pride when I 'matched' with someone whose
photo and image seemed appealing. Guardian Soulmates and Christian Connection invited me to sound clever with my words. At first I
enjoyed being on these apps, but then I began to experience the neg-
atives – unresponsive matches and unmet expectations feeling like a
rejection of my best self. 1 John is a short book of just five chapters in
which the Apostle John wrote to believers to whom he was particularly close, stressing the basic truths of the Christian faith in order to
comfort and encourage them. This scripture encompasses an under-
lying truth, which is that God loves us: 'See what great love the Father
has lavished on us, that we should be called children of God!' As
much as I experienced the adulation from peoples' affirming com-
ments and matches, they left me feeling less than when only empty
promises ensued. With God, we have unwavering assurance of his
love for us. John 3.16, one of the best-known passages in the Bible,
reads, 'For God so loved the world that he gave his one and only Son,
that whoever believes in him shall not perish but have eternal life.'

God knew us before we were born (Ps. 139.13–14) and he planned a great future for us (Jer. 29.11), no part of which is dependent on how photogenic or witty we are or how many countries we have travelled to. There are no empty promises here. He loves us, he loves us, he loves us. Whether or not we use dating apps, we need to be aware of our self-worth without them and remember that God always says 'Yes' to us. He always swipes right (metaphorically, of course).

LESSON 78

Age ain't nothing but . . .
half your age plus seven

Listen! My beloved!
   Look! Here he comes,
leaping across the mountains,
   bounding over the hills.
My beloved is like a gazelle or a young stag.
   Look! There he stands behind our wall,
gazing through the windows,
   peering through the lattice.

—Song of Songs 2.8–9 (NIV)

Aaliyah's '90s R&B song 'Age ain't nothing but a number', which tells
the story of a young girl wanting to be with an older man, seems less
innocent now that we have been given glimpses into the allegations
surrounding her music producer and one-time husband R Kelly.
While big age gaps have been common in older men and younger
women – especially in the Bible – it is becoming more commonly
accepted for older women to date younger men. Fish is nine years
older than me, and after our divorce, I dated someone four years
younger than me (probably seeking some sort of opposite experience.) He passed the 'half your age plus seven rule', but was the same
age as my little brother – which felt a bit weird – but we had so much
fun together; just being with him really lifted my spirits. I came
across this scripture in Song of Songs Chapter 2 verses 8–9 while
we were together, and when I read 'young stag', I thought of him
immediately (it even became his nickname for a while). There is so

much playfulness and joy in the passages here, and the descriptions of the way the lovers interacted resonated with me. We all know that relationships are hard work, but I think sometimes the importance of playfulness and attraction gets lost. Being with my older husband had made me lean more into the seriousness of life under the guise of 'growing up'. I had also assumed that an older partner would be more mature, but that isn't necessarily the case. In 1 Timothy 4.12, Paul writes to a younger apprentice Timothy and says, 'Don't let anyone look down on you because you are young.' While we might think that wisdom comes only with age, God provides examples in people like David defeating Goliath and Joseph becoming second in command in all of Egypt that show that he uses young people to achieve great things. With my young stag, the lightness of the relationship was a positive thing for me at the time, even leading to a ski season in the French Alps – one of the best things I've ever done. Clearly there is so much more to a person than their age might suggest, and we see in the Bible that God does not ID people before dishing out his wisdom. So don't write off those young stags; if you're open to it, you might be surprised!

LESSON 79

Opposites attract

Then God said, 'Let there be light,' and there was light. And God saw that the light was good. Then he separated the light from the darkness. God called the light 'day' and the darkness 'night.' And evening passed and morning came, marking the first day.

—Genesis 1.3–5 (NLT)

I couldn't stop staring at a couple on the tube recently. They wore his and hers bowler hats, almost identical gold stacked wedding rings and matching brogues, and both emitted such effortless cool. While they were dressed the same, in looks they were polar opposites, and I caught myself wondering about their backstory. How and where did they meet? Were they immediately drawn to each other? It's often said that you should marry your best friend, but I think that can sometimes be interpreted as someone with whom we have loads in common; I've often fallen into that trap when using dating apps. Because you can be so prescriptive about what you're looking for, I got used to scrolling through the list of profiles until I saw something that mirrored my profile. But what if we should really be looking for a partner who will be our fit rather than our twin? In life, things that fit together are never actually the same. In card games, a winning pair is often formed of two different types, magnets only attract if they are opposing poles and most of us will be familiar with the Chinese philosophy of yin and yang which describes how seemingly contrary forces may actually be complementary. God created things in both pairs and opposites. There is light and dark, as in this scripture from Genesis, and as we see later in the book, land and water, male and female. These opposites complement each other, and we need both sides of each pair to make things work. If you are particularly shy, you may feel 'safe' with someone who is also happy not to engage with others unless strictly necessary, but then who will coax you out of your comfort zone and encourage you to try new things and meet new people? If you are hugely gregarious, a calmer partner may be just what you need to get some balance in your life so that you don't completely burn out. Finding our 'tribe' is something we are encouraged to do with our friends, but sometimes if you step out of that, you open yourself up to finding something or someone different – and as we can see, God works in opposites.

LESSON 80

Jesus is the cornerstone

See, I lay a stone in Zion,
    a chosen and precious cornerstone,
and the one who trusts in him
    will never be put to shame.

—1 Peter 2.6 (NIV)

I added this lesson at the very last minute, proof that these lessons are very much 'alive' as I go through this journey of learning and discovery. Maybe this one will resonate with you. At a relationship seminar I attended recently, we discussed the importance of knowing your triggers. For me, I am triggered by anything which smells of rejection. And if you have ever gone through a period of dating, it's possible you know what that feels like. And it's painful. The ground I thought I had reached while getting to know God and feeling secure in him following my divorce felt strong and solid. I no longer felt I needed a partner to be complete. But after countless episodes of being ghosted, ignored and passed over for someone else, I felt drained and despondent with the shame of rejection. Then last night, this scripture came to mind and God gave me this lesson. Explanations of this Bible passage explore the importance of the cornerstone in the building process. Once in place, the cornerstone gives strength to the whole building and helps it to fulfil its purpose. When I think about my past relationships, both good and bad, I realize that none of them have fully provided that structural support for my being and purpose. And that's fine, because it's not their job. Holding up a building is not easy, and if we build the foundation of our very being on a 'stone' not built for it, i.e., our latest bae, however strong they may appear, they and we will always fail. The job of supporting us, helping us to stand up in difficulty and keeping us from collapsing, belongs to Jesus. *He* is the cornerstone in our lives. It's easy to forget this when we go through difficult dating experiences, but regardless, God is teaching me to remember that when we trust in his carefully chosen cornerstone, we will never be put to shame.

Section Nine

Lessons from health

A waiter once questioned my order as I asked for garlic bread for starters and a full-size pizza for my main. He politely suggested that my friend and I share since the pizza would be big enough for the two of us. Mildly outraged, we made a jokey bet with him that if I finished it, he would pay for our meal. This waiter didn't know me, my appetite or how competitive I am, so he did end up owing us that bill (but I felt pretty sick afterwards).

This is one example of how I have neglected this important area of my life: health. I have a tendency to overeat – sharing bags mean nothing to me – and even though I'm usually left feeling bloated and sick, it doesn't stop me the next time. And it's not just my physical health: my mental, emotional and financial health have all taken a back seat as I plough through this journey called life.

John 14.27 says that you should not 'let your heart be troubled, not let it be fearful'. 1 Corinthians 6.19–20 reads, 'Don't you know that your body is a temple of the Holy Spirit...so you must honour God with your body.' And we read this in Proverbs 22:7: 'The rich rule over the poor, and the borrower is servant to the lender.' This section is full of the lessons God has taught me about health in its wider sense, and while I'm still very much learning, I believe they can help us all on our way to being healthier temples for God.

LESSON 81

Your body is a temple

> Do you not know that your bodies are temples of the Holy
> Spirit, who is in you, whom you have received from God? You
> are not your own; you were bought at a price. Therefore honour
> God with your bodies.
>
> —1 Corinthians 6.19–20 (NIV)

In my teens and early 20s, I could generally eat huge portions of my
favourite foods (pizza, pasta, Thai), go to sleep full and wake up with
a flat stomach. Needless to say, I took full advantage of that. In my
mid-20s, I began to have problems digesting gluten (causing frequent
urination) and dairy (which resulted in flu-like symptoms). For the
first time in my life, I had to really pay attention to what I was eating.
At Sunday School, I was taught about this scripture in 1 Corinthians
in reference to sex: 'Do you not know that your bodies are temples of
the Holy Spirit, who is in you, whom you have received from God?'
It was only in adulthood that I saw how this also applies to how we
treat our bodies in terms of food and drink. I had been abusing my
body with food for years, and my symptoms were the result of that
destructive cycle. A colleague suggested I try a variation of the 'Daniel Fast'. Named after a period of mourning in which he ate no rich
foods, this was the diet Daniel followed in Daniel 1:12 whereby he
ate only vegetables and water in order to persuade the king's chief of
staff that he would be stronger and more clear-headed without the
rich food assigned him by the king (spoiler: he was). The vegetable-
based diet I pursued eschewed all meat, refined sugars, salt, alcohol
and coffee. It might sound extreme, but after the dip of the first few

days, I had more energy, my skin was clearer and my limited options made food shops much quicker. While it was difficult, as someone who loves to eat out, I knew that my body had hugely benefitted. I was also able to recognize the emotional value I had attached to food – that stuffing my face until completely full was a way of pushing down the emotions I found hard to deal with. A friend of mine who also does this explained it as her way of 'self-harming with food'. I had never really thought about it before, but if we are stuffing ourselves with food we know doesn't make us feel good afterwards, then we are harming our bodies. But when we are honest with ourselves and have these sugary and salty crutches removed, we can face God with those struggles instead, opening up space for a newfound 'hunger' for God.

LESSON 82

Lessons from the slopes

Dear friend, I hope all is well with you and that you are as healthy in body as you are strong in spirit.

—3 John 2 (NLT)

It wasn't until leaving London to do a ski season in the French Alps that I realized just how unhealthy my life had become. I was nervous when I first read the job spec for my role leading a team in the running of a ski chalet which could hold up to 40 new guests each week. Past seasonnaires, as they are known, revealed stories of 18-hour days, demanding guests and hands destroyed by the constant washing and cleaning. I was an editor, used to sitting down for most of the day, and I've always hated the cold so it was a hard adjustment. However, six weeks in, I had adapted to the routine and started to see the benefits of my new work. I became physically stronger from shovelling snow and negotiating the slopes and, after the initial shock of altitude, found my skin and hair flourished from the mountain water and air. The company I worked with was Christian-run, meaning I got to spend time with Christians from all walks of life; there's something very special about praying and worshipping together in full view of the unspoiled mountains that God created. This scripture in 3 John is the opening of a personal letter from the Apostle John to his friend Gaius. The simple greeting is akin to today's 'Hope you're well', but while we may proffer that greeting rhetorically, John writes to encourage his friend in his work, knowing that a strong body and spirit are key components for both worship and wellness (Rom. 12.1–2). Encouraged by how well I felt in the Alps, when I returned to

London, I took up regular exercise, stopped reading work emails on the weekend and joined a church small group which met weekly. These changes had hugely positive impacts on my physical, mental and spiritual health, and they didn't take much to start. Whether you live in the city or country, you can find ways to introduce balance into your life so that you really are both 'healthy in mind' and 'strong in spirit', putting yourself in the best position to serve God.

LESSON 83

Food served with love

For the whole law can be summed up in this one command: Love your neighbour as yourself.

—Galatians 5.14 (NLT)

My friend Rachael says you can love people through the food you make for them, and I agree. I love opening up my home to share food, drink and the occasional dancing. When I first moved outside the M25, I invited friends over to experience 'Christmas in the country', and we made mulled wine and traipsed over the Chilterns in Hunter wellies and Barbours like the parody of country-bound city dwellers we were. I've had some of the most open conversations over the dining table with friends as we talk deep into the night with no one rushing us to pay the bill and leave, with the benefits to our physical and mental health when we share (good) food with other people clear to see. Now that I'm in my own place, I frequently have people pop in for an impromptu dinner; one lesson I've learnt is to be ready with a quick and easy 'feel your way' recipe to satisfy last-minute guests. I can't remember what I was trying to make when I discovered this dish, but it was a happy accident. You can add cuts of meat or mushroom to bulk it up, but this has been a winner with meat-eaters and vegans alike.

My Accidental Risotto

Ingredients

- Brown basmati rice (gives a nice nutty taste)
- Beef or large vine tomatoes
- Red, yellow and green bell peppers
- Red onion
- Seasoning – salt, pepper, curry powder (or ground turmeric and cumin), garlic granules, chilli flakes
- Coconut oil or rapeseed oil
- Fresh vegetable stock (optional)

Method

- Cook rice according to instructions on packet
- Sauté chopped onions in oil and add roughly chopped tomatoes
- Add sliced peppers and continue to cook on low heat
- Add the cooked rice, seasoning and vegetable stock
- Turn up the heat and let the rice absorb the liquid for about 20–25 minutes while stirring
- Remove from heat when rice is more like risotto and less like soup
- And serve!

LESSON 84

No notifications today

But Jesus often withdrew to the wilderness for prayer.
—Luke 5.16 (NLT)

One of the benefits of being single is that I can go 'off grid' whenever I like. Not everyone wants to be unreachable, but for me, sometimes the constant flow of communication gets too much and I find my creativity just gets blocked (admittedly, this can also happen when I watch too much reality TV – I can feel my brain getting dumbed down with every second). The first time I forced myself to switch off from the outside world, I felt bereft. As a single person, your interactions with others are even more important than if you live with and are surrounded by people all the time, and I definitely felt the FOMO. By the second or third time, however, my mind and body felt healthier and less stressed. This short nine-word sentence in Luke 5.16 is significant because solitude was a consistent practice in Jesus' life as he spent time with his Father. In Mark 1.35 we read that 'Jesus got up and went out to an isolated place to pray'; in Matthew 14.13 when he heard the news that John the Baptist had been killed, 'he left in a boat to a remote area to be alone'; in Luke 6.12 before he chose the 12 disciples, 'Jesus went up on a mountain to pray, and he prayed all night'; and he cried out in distress in the Garden of Gethsemane in Luke 22.39–44. I didn't realize I was missing out on hearing God's voice until I quieted my life to listen for it. For that first successful off-grid practice, I turned off all screens and spent the time cooking, reading and doing what a friend of mine said her hippy Christian grandma referred to as 'soaking' – lying on the floor listening to worship music and seeing what thoughts or ideas are brought up in the process. Going off-grid is a practice I return to often, especially when the stresses of life start to affect my mental health, or I'm struggling to hear God's voice or even my own. Jesus drew his strength from his Father, and John 15.5 tells us that Jesus is the vine, we are the branches, so we too need to spend time in prayer so that we can draw our strength and health from him.

LESSON 85

Facing your finances

She makes sure her dealings are profitable;
her lamp burns late into the night.

—Proverbs 31.18 (NLT)

Thankfully, many women these days will be in charge of their own finances. For me, my first experience of credit was a store card from the shoe shop Faith during my first year of university. I used it with joyful abandon until I realized how much interest I was paying. I paid it off as soon as I could, and this experience, luckily, put me off accepting any more credit while I was studying. While I saw credit cards as intimidating loan sharks, I began to see my overdraft as a friendly aunt in comparison, letting me dip in for some extra cash with a knowing smile. There are many references to money in the Bible (Ecclesiastes 5.10; Proverbs 13.11; Hebrews 13.5), but I chose this one because it is about a woman; even at the patriotic time of writing, this verse did not negate the responsibility of women to seek financial health. I also love that this chapter is attributed to a king who was taught the message by his mother. The description of the 'Proverbs 31 woman' who 'makes sure her dealings are profitable' is an inspiration for us to make sure our hard-earned money works for us, and my take from 'her lamp burns late into the night' is that there is long-lasting value in her investments. When I finally sat down with a financial adviser, I realized how much of my debt I could be repaying rather than transferring the minimum amount each month and spending the rest on daily coffee and trendy pop-up restaurants. At first I couldn't see how I would survive if I tripled my repayments, but nine months later, I had completely paid off my debt and was back on the road to financial health. With the money going out as soon as my salary came in, I didn't have time to miss it and simply *had* to live on the remaining income. The worry of debt can hang over us like a cloud, so the sooner we get rid of it the better. Similarly, the love of money can also cast a cloud over us if we let it become an insatiable obsession; balance is key. So sign up for emails from websites like moneysavingexpert.com and money.co.uk for ideas on how to be savvy with your spending. With the many references to money in the Bible, this is an area of health God deems as important for us to keep on top of.

LESSON 86

How to spend
a pre-payday weekend

Then the LORD said to Elijah, 'Go and live in the village of Zarephath, near the city of Sidon. I have instructed a widow there to feed you.'

So he went to Zarephath. As he arrived at the gates of the village, he saw a widow gathering sticks, and he asked her, 'Would you please bring me a little water in a cup?' As she was going to get it, he called to her, 'Bring me a bite of bread, too.'

But she said, 'I swear by the LORD your God that I don't have a single piece of bread in the house. And I have only a handful of flour left in the jar and a little cooking oil in the bottom of the jug. I was just gathering a few sticks to cook this last meal, and then my son and I will die.'

But Elijah said to her, 'Don't be afraid! Go ahead and do just what you've said, but make a little bread for me first. Then use what's left to prepare a meal for yourself and your son. For this is what the LORD, the God of Israel, says: There will always be flour and olive oil left in your containers until the time when the LORD sends rain and the crops grow again!'

So she did as Elijah said, and she and Elijah and her family continued to eat for many days. There was always enough flour and olive oil left in the containers, just as the LORD had promised through Elijah.

—1 Kings 17.8–16 (NLT)

It seems the norm for many of us to almost expect to be running on empty towards the end of the month as payday approaches, and there may be one weekend in the month where we have little to no money to do anything at all, living in a state of anxiety and 'never enough'. In this scripture God shows his provision as the widow prepares food for a stranger, before herself and her son. God blesses what she has, and she ends up with a healthy dose of plenty. We live in a very purchase-driven society where it is tempting to rely on credit to fill the gap between what we have and what we want. While the widow's metaphorical bank account was literally at zero and ours might only be low until a future date, we need to know that God will always help us make good use of what we already have, just like he did for the widow, and that we can always live in an abundance of faith. Encouraged by this scripture, one pre-payday weekend, I decided to get creative with what I had. Having run out of shaving cream, I utilized hair conditioner; when I got hungry, I made up dishes using whatever food I had, and I Googled how to make my own winter skin body cream; I ended up using olive oil, coconut oil – both of which I cook with and already had – and a random pot of beeswax I discovered in the cupboard. It was brilliant and I still use that formula today. By the end of the weekend, I felt really pleased with how productive I'd been – without going overdrawn or using money I didn't have. One of the names for God is Jehovah-Jireh, which means 'The Lord will provide' (Gen. 22.14), and although this example may sound a little trivial to some, it is indicative of a much bigger point: when we trust him with that handful of flour and little bit of cooking oil left in the jar, we'll see that he always does.

LESSON 87

Understanding January

The LORD said to Moses at Mount Sinai, 'Speak to the Israelites and say to them: "When you enter the land I am going to give you, the land itself must observe a sabbath to the LORD. For six years sow your fields, and for six years prune your vineyards and gather their crops. But in the seventh year the land is to have a year of sabbath rest, a sabbath to the LORD. Do not sow your fields or prune your vineyards. Do not reap what grows of itself or harvest the grapes of your untended vines. The land is to have a year of rest. Whatever the land yields during the sabbath year will be food for you – for yourself, your male and female servants, and the hired worker and temporary resident who live among you, as well as for your livestock and the wild animals in your land. Whatever the land produces may be eaten."'

—Leviticus 25.1–7 (NIV)

January is often a dreaded time. Bills for the Christmas period start to come in, and the reality of a long month until payday looms drearily. I find it frustrating that we basically write off a whole month just because reality hits us harder than in any other, with no one really wanting to do anything – as if our January days weren't also God's gift. I shared these frustrations with my friend Kate, and she suggested that we might consider January a dedicated month of quiet and stillness – an anticipated period of rest and hibernation while we nurse ourselves back to health – in all areas. Her suggestion reminded me of history lessons in school and hearing about the way farmland used to be treated, including the necessary leaving of the land 'fallow' for one year out of every four. This allowed the land a healthy 'rest' as it regained its natural nutrients and was best placed to support the next lot of produce the following year. Applied rest is a concept I was used to as a Christian observing Sabbath days, but as a city girl, my agricultural knowledge was somewhat limited. In my research I found this scripture in Leviticus where God tells Moses that the people of Israel are to give the land itself a break, and he calls it a 'sabbath year'. While the people are permitted to eat from the land, they are not allowed to farm it so that it too can rest. I realized that what Kate had said made complete sense. Christmas is often the busiest time of year; we are socializing, shopping, drinking and eating in copious amounts, all in the name of celebrating the season. So it makes sense for January to be our down time where we let our minds, bodies and wallets rest and we can be restored back to health. We have gotten used to a 24/7 lifestyle but God prescribed rest for a reason, and starting with a healthy mind, body and bank account really does make a better start to a fresh new year.

LESSON 88

When your hair is not your crown

Do not be anxious about anything, but in every situation, by prayer and petition, with thanksgiving, present your requests to God.

—Philippians 4.6 (NIV)

During my engagement, my home life was pretty difficult, so when I went to the GP with hair loss, I already knew the cause: stress. There was a coin-shaped patch of completely bald skin that I just couldn't seem to cover up as my emotional ill health manifested in the physical. While I managed with braids for our wedding day, the alopecia persisted into life with my new husband. He was always very reassuring about how I looked, but as women we often hear that our hair is our crown, so I felt as though I had failed to measure up. Thankfully, the freedom to pray to God about anything is here in this scripture. Paul wrote these words as a source of encouragement to some friends in Philippi, 'Do not be anxious about anything, but in every situation, by prayer and petition, with thanksgiving, present your requests to God.' I remember crying over my hair, just wanting it and this small part of my feminine identity back. I think he might have said it as a joke to show me he really would love me anyway, but when Fish said, 'why don't you just cut it all off?', something in me clicked. I went online and scrolled through hundreds of pictures of women with shaved heads to try and understand how I would look, but like taking a picture of a celebrity into the hairdresser, you never really know what it will look like on you until you take the plunge. Looking back over pictures from that time, I can't believe I had any hesitation; I felt amazing. Embracing my new look, I kept my head shaved for about two years and modelled more during that time than any other period in my life. My prayer was for God to restore my scalp to full physical health, but he focused on my emotional health instead. Lots of us might be used to hiding behind our physical 'beauty', but I didn't have a choice. Cutting my hair made me vulnerable and, in turn, made me much more confident in exposing it.

LESSON 89

Not world peace prayers

Take delight in the LORD,
  and he will give you the desires of your heart.

—Psalm 37.4 (NIV)

God has blessed me with the very special gift of not being able to fit into regular-sized bras. With limited options in most of the stores around as I was growing up, I spent my teens in horridly unflattering plain black or white sports bras. I know some people think of big boobs as a positive thing, but as an active teen, I was always self-conscious about mine. More brands began to stock wider size ranges as I entered adulthood, and when I discovered a brand which worked practically, as well as aesthetically, I became a dedicated ambassador. With its high price point, I tend to only shop there during the sales, and I was elated when a piece I had admired from afar finally received a drastic price cut – but they didn't have my size. Deflated at my always less-than-simple bra search, I saw this scripture from the book of Psalms on a card my mum had given me. Psalm 37 is attributed to King David, and he speaks to us of his experience that if you 'take delight in the Lord...he will give you the desires of your heart,' so I decided to take my petition to God. In all my years of being a believer, I realized it was the first time I would be praying for something overtly trivial that would benefit only me. But God reminds us that he cares about each and every 'only me' in Luke 12.7: 'And the very hairs on your head are all numbered.' Someone explained to me that this scripture doesn't mean that God knows how many strands of hair we have on our heads; it means that each one has a number, and he knows all of those numbers. I think Christians often have a hard time believing that God actually cares about our wellbeing if we are not drastically sick or needy, but this should remind us how intimately he knows and cares about how we feel about ourselves. When I finally found my size, I danced around my room with delight and thanked God for a very personal answer to prayer. While my petition would not have been featured on a list of country priorities, God showed me that we are always a priority to him. Next time you want to make a personal request to God, don't hesitate to follow Psalm 116.2: 'Because he bends down to listen, I will pray as long as I have breath!'

LESSON 90

Be nice

Get rid of all bitterness, rage, anger, harsh words, and slander, as well as all types of evil behaviour.

—Ephesians 4.31 (NLT)

I once read this analysis of social media: Instagram is a show-off, Twitter is bitchy and Facebook is dumb. It's harsh but as a frequent Twitter user, I can agree with its assigned characteristic. While the premise for Facebook is on connecting with friends, on Twitter, you can have a 'conversation' with literally anyone without having liked or followed them. It baffles me when users actively follow people they disagree with just so they can shut down every tweet they post, and while there are plenty of users who support each other, there are also plenty who do the opposite with a tone that is seriously unkind. This scripture is from a letter written to the Church in Ephesus by Paul. The heading of this section in my NLT Bible reads: 'Living as children of Light'. Paul encourages believers to stand out from the Gentiles who have 'closed their minds against God' and who 'eagerly practice every kind of impurity' (vv. 18, 19). He tells them to 'let the Spirit renew your thoughts and attitudes. Put on your new nature, created to be like God – truly righteous and holy.' (vv. 23–24). Because I love words and admire those who use them cleverly, I forget that quick-wittedness can easily slip into bitchy undertones, and the warning against using 'harsh words and slander' in verse 31 really convicted me. Social media has been blamed for a lot of ill mental health and bullying and has been known to contribute to suicide. I often find myself close to pledging my allegiance to a bitchy comment or meme with the simple click on the heart icon, without even thinking about how the original poster will feel; it can be easy to jump on the bandwagon and get involved. But when I read verse 30, 'And do not bring sorrow to God's Holy Spirit by the way you live,' I remembered that God does not just want us to be 'good'; he calls us to be holy (2 Timothy 1.9), and that means refusing to engage in behaviour that can negatively impact another's mental health and to instead seek the kind of life that mirrors him.

Section Ten

Lessons from standing

Someone once told me if you don't stand for something, you'll fall for anything. Sometimes it feels like there's a lot of pressure to have an opinion on something. But in my experience, it's wiser to keep quiet about something you're not that fussed about. It's fine to bow out of having a strong opinion on something if that means you are freer to work out what is important to you. Save your energy for standing for the things that matter.

What are you passionate about? Animal welfare? The environment? The gender pay gap? We can use our energy better when focused on a few good things rather than spreading them thinly over whatever happens to be topical at the time.

Then, of course, there is standing for something in the storm – when it feels like everything comes to get you and knocks you off course.

This section, like the book it finds itself in, is all about standing. The lessons are born from things I stand up for, stick to and protect – and some things I have learned are not so important, especially to God. These may be lessons God has taught me, but I'm not attempting to rewrite the Bible; that's still standing good enough as it is. And I'm sure you have countless other stories to share about how you are standing up and sticking to the passions God has filled you with. In my experience, it is in sharing the stories of 'standing firm' in who God is and who he has made us to be that encourages others to do the same. I hope that, in some way, God has used this book and the messy lessons held within it to encourage you to stand up and stand firm in fighting for a 'full life' with him.

LESSON 91

Let 'Judge Judy' do her job

You, therefore, have no excuse, you who pass judgment on someone else, for at whatever point you judge another, you are condemning yourself, because you who pass judgment do the same things.

—Romans 2.1 (NIV)

Judge Judy is an American reality court show presided over by a retired Manhattan family court judge. Judge Judy Sheindlin is known for her no-nonsense attitude and witty retorts, but she actually is a judge, unlike me whose perfectionist ways often make me feel like I am. Growing up in a teetotal household, I was never really interested in alcohol and managed to get through three whole years of university with zero hangovers. I would roll my eyes at girls throwing up on the side of the road and irritably push away the drunk dancers swaying their way through, and often into, the crowd on the dance floor. Stories of friends waking up with no memory of the previous night's events or covered in their own vomit received the same condemnation from me. I labelled them irresponsible, feckless, immature. We are advised in the New Testament, 'Do not get drunk on wine, which leads to debauchery. Instead, be filled with the Spirit' (Eph. 5.18), with similar exhortation in Galatians 5.19–21. So maybe my disdain for this specific sin of choice would be justified, but a truth universally acknowledged is that if you judge others, you will be judged (Luke 6.37), and the act of judging, as we see here in Romans, is something God frowns upon because when we judge, we are trying to stand in place of God. God judges what he sees in the heart – the truth – which is information we are not always privy to: 'Now we know that God's judgment against those who do such things is based on truth.' (Romans 2.2) Who really knows what is going on in the lives of those we see around us 'sinning' in their drunkenness or misspelled texts? My comeuppance came when I went to a party with a really cool girl and, intimidated, I drank way too much in a bid to try to relax. I got so drunk she ended up having to take me home. I woke up the next day with my sick all over the side of my bed and carpet. It's amazing how quickly I turned my judgement in on myself. Standing up for what you believe in is fine, but only when it is exemplified by your own behaviour. God teaches us that judging someone else is never part of our job, so let's leave that to him.

LESSON 92

Women united

Therefore encourage one another and build each other up, just as in fact you are doing.

—1 Thessalonians 5.11 (NIV)

I've been known to do a double take or even run after a woman on the street to tell her how good she looks, often with friends of both genders looking on in confusion. It's perhaps obvious, but I rarely do the same with men. For starters, I rarely see men who stand out enough for me to point it out, and second, it's hard to do without coming across as having an ulterior motive. For the record, I very much like men; I just think we women have so much more capacity to be beautiful, so I make a point of standing up to say so. It is often said that women dress for other women rather than men, and I think to some extent this is true; it means a lot more to me if a woman tells me my outfit looks good than if a man does. But this is about more than just complimenting each other on our looks. It has changed drastically (for good) in recent years, but historically I would say women have not necessarily lifted each other up as we should. I recently read about a family in which the young teenage daughter had been raped and became pregnant. Culturally, an unwed mother brought shame into the family, and her mother kicked her out. It was her father who helped the girl get support and brought her back to the bosom of her family. I was shocked when I read this; surely the mother would have been the one to understand her daughter's plight. But it seems that here, a patriarchal system played a part in negative influencing. We see similarities in today's workplaces where attempts to fill gender quotas have meant we might not necessarily pull each other up because it might 'threaten' our own spot – it sees us pitted against each other. This is mirrored in biblical text with relationships between Sarah and Hagar and Leah and Rachel becoming fraught as they negotiated the value placed on women based on their ability to have children. This scripture in 1 Thessalonians was part of a letter from Paul to young believers in Thessalonica. They were experiencing persecution, and he was encouraging them to seek unity in Christ and support each other. Today we are seeing a rise in the value placed on women, and this is important; what is also important is that we keep pulling each other up as we each see platforms open to us. I'm not saying that we shouldn't pull up men and vice versa, but the imbalance in this area means that right now, there is a need for women to stand up for other women, doing as Paul says: 'encourage each other and build each other up.'

LESSON 93

Righteous anger

Jesus entered the temple courts and drove out all who were buying and selling there. He overturned the tables of the money changers and the benches of those selling doves. 'It is written' he said to them, '"My house will be called a house of prayer", but you are making it "a den of robbers."'

—Matthew 21.12–13 (NIV)

I think there's often a conditioning in society that women should be gentle and submissive. Loud voices and argumentative tones feel out of keeping with this kind of temperament – so does this mean as women we shouldn't get angry? I struggled with this for a long time and would do almost anything to push down feelings of irritation and injustice, wanting to be seen as agreeable and easygoing. I was prone to more bouts of anger when I was younger – one of which was hitting someone with a lacrosse stick (off-field) – but I thought becoming a Christian meant being reticent and complicit, and so that's what I tried to become: anger was a negative emotion that needed to be squashed. But there's a very clear picture of the calm character of Jesus 'losing it' in the Bible, which reveals anger's importance in standing up for what is right. The temple, a place of peace, was being completely misappropriated by opportunists who were using it as an open market. Jesus, angry at the way a place of worship was being treated as a business, completely tore down the stalls, probably breaking valuables in the process, and told everyone to get out. In another passage in Mark 3.1–6, we read that Jesus gets angry at the Pharisees for their disapproval of him healing a man on the Sabbath (v. 5). When anger is over the mistreatment or malice of another, it is in keeping with the scripture in Psalm 82.3–4 to 'Defend the weak and the fatherless; uphold the cause of the poor and the oppressed. Rescue the weak and the needy; deliver them from the hand of the wicked.' Without someone standing up with this kind of righteous anger, we would probably not have the vote for women today, and it might still be legal for ethnic minorities living in the UK to be treated as second-class citizens. Most, if not all, of the advocacy work taking place today has come from a place of righteous anger, and it can be detrimental to try and suppress it. Obviously, there are things we should turn the other cheek on, but when something really stirs up a feeling of injustice, it's good to remember that there is such a thing as righteous anger and it's our duty to ask God to help us stand up and do something about it.

LESSON 94

Ask for what you want!

Keep on asking, and you will receive what you ask for. Keep on seeking, and you will find. Keep on knocking, and the door will be opened to you.

—Matthew 7.7 (NLT)

I've already mentioned that I'm a bit of a people pleaser; I hate to feel I might have disappointed someone by something I have or haven't done. But it has taken me a long time to get to a position where I feel comfortable asking for what *I* want. My favourite aunt observed that when I'm in relationships, I'm particularly giving and seem to doubt I deserve as much as my partner. Not that I've dated men who were particularly overbearing, but she sensed that in an argument I would rather compromise to his benefit than mine. I didn't realize how true this was until she said it. I sometimes think there is something about being a woman which means we are predisposed or culturally encouraged to please. A while ago, I watched a ridiculous reality TV show based in the U.S. which followed American citizens and their overseas partners as they raced against time to get married within 90 days in order to be presented with a residency visa for the non-U.S. citizen. One episode showed a demanding Russian fiancée who frequently threw tantrums when her American husband-to-be didn't give her what she wanted. Clearly, we were meant to be outraged at her behaviour, but I noticed that her fiancé had quite obviously been complying with her demands and they hadn't put him off. It's hard to say what really goes on when the cameras are turned off, but what I did see was a woman who wasn't afraid to stand up and ask for exactly what she wanted. This scripture shows Jesus teaching about effective prayer, and he really encourages us here to ask for what we want with a very simple cause-and-effect formula. Standing up for what we want can seem daunting, and women often don't do it – from our bosses in the boardroom to our husbands in the bedroom, there seems to be a reluctance to ask. But Jesus goes on to say later in verses 9–11, 'You parents – if your children ask for a loaf of bread, do you give them a stone instead? Or if they ask for a fish, do you give them a snake? Of course not! So if you sinful people know how to give good gifts to your children, how much more will your heavenly Father give good gifts to those who ask him.' In my experience, God will give what I *need* as a priority over what (I think) I *want,* which is testament to his goodwill towards us. But either way, God says that we can go to him for the good gifts he desires to give us. Just don't be afraid to ask.

LESSON 95

Superwoman

Adam named his wife Eve, because she would become the mother of all the living.

—Genesis 3.20 (NIV)

Do you know how powerful you are as a woman? When I think about the stuff we have to go through, I'm honestly amazed at our day-to-day existence. For example, while I concede that men are generally stronger than us physically, would they cope with seven days (sometimes longer) of uncontrollable bleeding every month? Women learn to keep calm and carry on no matter what we have to do during that time, not to speak of the hormonal rages and crushing pain that can often accompany it. When I was pregnant, Fish bought a baby book and we were fascinated reading about the changes the body goes through and how the baby grows inside a woman, with our bodies knowing exactly what to do and when. Seeing other women further along, standing strong and continuing to do life with this new one growing inside, was fascinating. I cringe as I recall a hot yoga class with my then eight-months-pregnant teacher asking us why we kept pausing during the practice – 'If I can do it, you can do it too!' Our first insight into procreation of humans is in Genesis 3.16: 'I will make your pains in childbearing very severe; with painful labour you will give birth to children.' We already read in Genesis 1.28 that God has commanded humans to 'be fruitful', but we don't know what that looked like before Adam and Eve ate the apples and ruined it all. Either way, when I read this scripture in Genesis 3.20, I read it as a blessing. Adam, the first human creation, names his helper as the one 'would become the mother of all the living'. The name 'Eve' is thought to originate from the Hebrew name Chawwah, which was derived from the Hebrew word chawah meaning 'to breathe' or the related word chayah meaning 'to live'. It struck me as incredible, reading this, how blessed we are as women, to have this creative ability from the breath of God, to help give and nurture life to another human being. Before this, only God was known to be able to 'give life', but when Eve gave birth to her first child, she said in Genesis 4.1, 'With the help of the Lord I have brought forth a man.' It's a gift that, for some reason, was not given to men, and I think it important for us to remember this: whether we use it or not, if we are ever feeling like the 'lesser sex', remember that every single day you are standing strong as superwoman.

LESSON 96

We need men too

There is neither Jew nor Gentile, neither slave nor free, nor is there male and female, for you are all one in Christ Jesus.

—Galatians 3.28 (NIV)

For years I worked for a charity which focused on empowering women and girls, and one of the frequent reports back from projects in remote villages across Africa and Asia was the same – we need to stand with men to get them on board too. It's all very well, they reported, to focus on empowering women and girls, to inform them of their rights, to care for and educate them. But when they tried to operate in this new way of thinking, they soon defaulted back to the position of second-class citizens because those conversations on change had been limited to women only. As far as the men were aware, the patriarchy was alive and well. Here in the West, I feel the same thing is happening where women are being told they're strong, independent and can do anything they want to do – all true, well and good things. But has anyone passed this memo to the men? Have they been invited to see the benefits of this new way of being? Or have they just been relegated to the side, confused at the way society is changing around them without any way of navigating it – and should we even care? The above scripture in Galatians addresses more debating on how we should live, with God making clear his word is for everyone: 'nor is there male and female, for you are all one in Christ Jesus.' However they were living at the time, this was the call for believers to be aware of how God viewed his people, and this 'new' sense of equality would have taken time to adjust to, for both men and women. Society has made huge strides since then to raise the profile and agency of women. But since no previously marginalized group has been able to effect such drastic change themselves, frustrating as it might be, we need the patriarchy standing with us because, as Paul writes in 1 Corinthians 11.11, 'in the Lord woman is not independent of man, nor is man independent of woman' and later in 11.12, 'For as woman came from man, so also man is born of woman. But everything comes from God.' God has purposed for us to need each other, so it's imperative that we stand together with men to effect important changes towards equality for everyone.

LESSON 97

The lost art of letter writing

See what large letters I use as I write to you with my own hand!
—Galatians 6.11 (NIV)

When I was younger, I was always writing letters. I wrote thank-you letters to family friends and relatives who gave me gifts; I wrote letters of discontent to Walkers when there was no salt sachet in my Salt 'n' Shake; I wrote letters to other children I met on holiday and as I got older, I wrote letters of application for jobs and courses. My mum encouraged me to write these, partly, I think, because she spotted an early talent for writing but also because in writing I was able to be more coherent in my thoughts. I'm much more confident now, but back then, gathering my thoughts on paper helped me stand up for things I believed in when I couldn't find the right words to speak. These days, while I mostly do my 'letter' writing by email, there is something about the solid nature of letters which causes me to revert back to writing when I feel I have something important to say. In biblical times, although not everyone was literate, plenty of communication took place by letters, which placed higher importance on their existence. Letters were written to communicate between enemies in battle, to prelude a guest's arrival and to impart knowledge and/or instruction to a group of people. The letters in the New Testament were imperative for the people who received them, as the Galatians, the Thessalonians, the Corinthians and the other churches to whom Paul sent letters were encouraged and blessed by his words and wisdom. Some of them helped clear up issues they were having (Galatians 3.5), and others encouraged new believers in their faith

(Ephesians 2:13). While a message relayed verbally might have been helpful, written words stand alone – there is no tone of voice to mis-interpret meaning – and seem to carry more weight. This intro to the last part of Paul's letter in Galatians begins with a strong call to pay attention, 'See what large letters I use as I write to you with my own hand!' Paul is about to impart some important advice (on the misunderstanding around circumcision which was part of Jewish law) and is reminding the recipients that it is him writing to them – a Jew well-versed in Jewish law, not a Gentile who might hijack the discussion as an excuse to avoid circumcision. A letter is direct, not a third-party communication, no matter how it is delivered, and I've found that communicating difficult issues in letters helps give the other person time to think about their reply rather than respond (often defensively) on the spot, as well as negating the expectation to respond at all as with emails or texts. So even if we write them just to make sense of how we are feeling, we can draw on Paul's example of how letters can help us metaphorically stand up as we use our words for good.

LESSON 98

Protect your dreams

The wise store up knowledge,
　　but the mouth of a fool invites ruin.

—Proverbs 10.14 (NIV)

It has long been a dream of mine to build my own house. Before house programmes monopolized Channel 4, I imagined being able to create my own space with self-designed features unique to the building. This hasn't happened yet, and as I write this, is unlikely to any time soon, but it remains on my 'bucket list'. I'm sure lots of other people want to build their own home, just as there are many people who want to write a book. But for various reasons, not everyone will, and I think that one of the reasons for this might be sharing your dreams with the wrong people. At work one day, my colleague and I were having lunch at our desks when he glanced over at my screen and asked what I had been looking at. I had been scrolling through images of split-level apartments in a particularly wealthy area of London so I could get ideas from the layout and design eked out in the often difficult spaces in the city. Before I could reply, he laughed in disbelief, 'Primrose Hill? Well, that's never going to happen, is it?' I know he wasn't being mean, just a true realist – but his words still planted a seed of doubt in me, and it made me wonder: had I shared that dream too soon? This short gem of a passage in the book of Proverbs is advice which suggests just that, 'The wise store up knowledge, but the mouth of a fool invites ruin.' Sometimes, God reveals things about our future that are for us alone. In Daniel 8.26 the angel Gabriel shares a vision with Daniel and then

217

says, 'This vision about the 2,300 evenings and mornings is true. But none of these things will happen for a long time, so keep this vision a secret.' Not everything we hear from God needs to be heard by other people. Sometimes God reveals things for the purpose of them being known and shared with others, but the 'knowledge' referred to in this passage of Proverbs is the type that a wise person might keep to themselves. It can be tempting, when we're excited about an idea or a project, to share it with people but at the risk of losing sight of your dream; the advice in this scripture is key to being careful with what you hold dear. You can stand up for what you believe by keeping your next move close to your chest, and don't let anyone put a dampener on your dream.

LESSON 99

God on our level

They went to Capernaum, and when the Sabbath came, Jesus went into the synagogue and began to teach. The people were amazed at his teaching, because he taught them as one who had authority, not as the teachers of the law. Just then a man in their synagogue who was possessed by an impure spirit cried out, 'What do you want with us, Jesus of Nazareth? Have you come to destroy us? I know who you are – the Holy One of God!'

'Be quiet!' said Jesus sternly. 'Come out of him!' The impure spirit shook the man violently and came out of him with a shriek. The people were all so amazed that they asked each other, 'What is this? A new teaching – and with authority! He even gives orders to impure spirits and they obey him.' News about him spread quickly over the whole region of Galilee.

—Mark 1.21–28 (NIV)

I've been told that I can come across as snobbish, which is not to say that I have an exceptionally high opinion of myself – it's just that I want to make sure everyone else does. Many Nigerians are proud by nature but also, living in a country which has historically looked down on people with my skin colour, I feel there are still certain stereotypes which pervade, and I don't like that – often overcompensating to stand up against them. My English builder once opened a conversation with, 'People like you and me' and went on to talk about growing up in poverty and lack of education. I instantly bristled, not identifying with either one of these instances, affronted that he had made such a big assumption. When Jesus began his ministry, many thought he was a prophet, not an unusual occupation at the time, and it appears he was not in a hurry to have his true identity revealed. In Mark 1.23, a man possessed by an evil spirit starts shouting, 'I know who you are – the Holy One sent from God!' but in verse 25, it says that Jesus cut him short. '"Be quiet!" said Jesus sternly. "Come out of him!" The impure spirit shook the man violently and came out of him with a shriek.' We read further on in verse 34, 'He also drove out many demons, but he would not let the demons speak because they knew who he was.' Had Jesus come as the king of the type people were used to, they would undoubtedly have treated him differently. He would have been kept separate from certain 'types' of people, the very people he chose to spend time with – those on the fringe of society. (Luke 14.12–14, Luke 15.1–2) He also would have been treated differently by those he was trying to help. Perhaps standing in finer robes and surrounded by soldiers, Jesus would have seemed unreachable, and many would not have felt free to come to him. Jesus came to break down the barrier between us and God, and he came in a form that would enable him to do that. Later, when he does confirm who he is, he says it so that people will believe and understand, not to make a statement about his standing in society. My builder wasn't trying to pigeonhole me in a way that would dictate who I was; he just thought that I would understand him, and I did, so in this case, why get offended if his perception helped him to communicate? Sometimes we do need to stand up for ourselves and refuse to be looked down on, but Jesus shows us that knowing who he is was enough for him, and so it must be enough for you and me.

LESSON 100

Lean into risk

Blessed is she who has believed that the Lord would fulfil his promises to her!

—Luke 1.45 (NIV)

When I was learning to ski, I was taught to lean my body forward in a way that might seem unnatural when hurtling yourself down the side of a mountain. It was uncomfortable and scary, and I frequently wanted to (and did) scream 'Stop!' to my long-suffering skis who were just doing their job. One of the hardest things for me as a Christian has been allowing God to take control, and what that looks like will be different for all of us. Mary and Joseph appear to have been an ordinary young couple who were engaged to be married when an angel of God sent a curveball into their relationship with the news that Mary would become pregnant with a child – that was not Joseph's (Luke 1.30–33). After the initial shock, she responded, "I am the Lord's servant...May your word to me be fulfilled.' At the time, this kind of risk could have caused her to be socially excluded – an unmarried woman, pregnant with a baby not fathered by her fiancé would have been a perilous position for her. But she accepted what the angel told her, 'The Holy Spirit will come on you, and the power of the Most High will overshadow you. So the holy one to be born will be called the Son of God.' She leaned into that risk. When she went to visit her cousin Elizabeth a few days later, we are shown that she had already fully embraced God's leadership in her life, whatever it might mean, as her cousin exclaims, 'Blessed is she who has believed that the Lord would fulfil his promises to her!' Mary's risk-taking made history. Now that I can ski, I realize that my instructor wasn't telling me to lean forward for the sake of it; he was telling me to move away from my position over the back of my skis, away from fear. Encouraging us away from fear (and away from the comfortable in the process) is where we ultimately find balance and stability. Mary might have been frightened at the news of what was to come, but by standing in a position of trust in God, she was blessed as the mother of Jesus and, despite the seemingly ominous circumstances, Joseph didn't abandon her as his wife (Matthew 1.20–25) but stood alongside her. Many things we face today involve some kind of risk-taking, but with God, what looks like risk is a place of safety in him, and like Mary, it is a place in which we can stand confidently, knowing that we will find God's true blessing for our lives. Fear of 'failure' or our perceived sense of failure can hem us in, but I hope this book in your hands has shown that if we let him, God uses anything and everything we go through to bring us into closer relationship with him. As I too learn this lesson, may you also be encouraged to join with Paul in Romans 8.28 in saying, 'And we know that in all things God works for the good of those who love him, who have been called according to his purpose.'

END.

WE HAVE A VISION

OF A WORLD IN

WHICH EVERYONE IS

TRANSFORMED BY

CHRISTIAN KNOWLEDGE

As well as being an award-winning publisher, SPCK is the oldest Anglican mission agency in the world.

Our mission is to lead the way in creating books and resources that help everyone to make sense of faith.

Will you partner with us to put good books into the hands of prisoners, great assemblies in front of schoolchildren and reach out to people who have not yet been touched by the Christian faith?

To donate, please visit www.spckpublishing.co.uk/donate or call our friendly fundraising team on 020 7592 3900.